MW01615189

STOP KILLING DEALS

HOW TO AVOID DEADLY ASSUMPTIONS AND ACHIEVE SALES EXCELLENCE

George Brontén
Founder and CEO, Membrain.com
With Fen Druadìn

ISBN: 978-91-519-4182-0 (paperback)
ISBN: 978-91-519-4183-7 (ebook)

Published by
Upstream Business Solutions AB
https://stop.killing.deals

george@membrain.com

Unmask and defeat the deadly assumptions at the root of your selling and gain competitive advantage by viewing sales through the lens of human nature.

Companies spend billions of dollars each year on sales training and technology, yet sales effectiveness keeps declining. Why? Because too many sales organizations operate on deadly assumptions that deny the essential human nature of their sales teams and their buyers.

Written by the CEO of a sales technology company, George Brontén, *Stop Killing Deals* defies convention by destroying the idea that CRM and other technology is the solution to all of the sales industry's problems. Instead, the book focuses on a human-centered way of building and maintaining world-class sales organizations that supports, rather than denies, the essential human nature of those who work within them.

In this quick and insightful read, you'll learn how to:

- Defeat the deal-killing monsters lurking in your buyer's subconscious

- Heal your organization and give your team what they need with sales enablement

- Align your strategy, process, and methodology to achieve scalable world-class sales performance

- Build your sales coaching around your sales process to generate exponential results within complex b2b sales environments

- Understand the essential humanity of your sales workforce enabling you to better recruit, train, and support the people on your team so you win more deals

- Turn your sales technology into your servant, not your master

The book contains links to a wealth of downloadable resources and tools to enable leaders to put its principles into practice right away. When you apply these principles and frameworks, you'll win more, and have more fun doing it!

WHAT OTHERS SAY ABOUT STOP KILLING DEALS

No other sales book pinpoints the problem like *Stop Killing Deals* does, and that's why it should be required reading for every b2b sales leader and CEO on the planet.

— **Deb Calvert, People First Productivity Solutions**

Why does the world need another book on sales? Because all that have come before it are just pieces of a larger puzzle. *Stop Killing Deals* takes a wide view of the sales force, putting human nature, sales process, CRM, and all the other pieces in their proper place.

— **Jason Jordan, author, *Cracking the Sales Management Code***

Stop Killing Deals digs into the bedrock of sales beliefs that are holding sellers back. George, in a straightforward and many times funny way, really nails the core issues that shape our sales culture today. The great news is that we can learn new ways of thinking and doing that lead to improved avenues for sales success. Anyone who is involved with selling should read this book.

— **Lisa D. Magnuson, Top Line Sales**

George Brontén's excellent new book is a practical guide to eliminating the avoidable errors that are preventing sales organizations from achieving their full potential.

— **Bob Apollo, Inflexion Point**

Imagine if the creator of a sales technology assessed the state of the industry and concluded that sales technology has caused more problems than it solves. In this book, the founder and CEO of a Sales Enablement CRM, George Brontén, shares how bad assumptions have made business the slave of technology. Then he presents a framework for achieving world-class performance by putting technology into its proper role as the servant of your people.

—**Tamara Schenk, Sales Enablement Evangelist, Analyst, Advisor, and Speaker**

George Brontén's fresh, daring, and insightful look into what's wrong with sales stands apart from every other book on sales. It's a fast read, it rings true, and you'll love the great stories he included for context.

—**Dave Kurlan, Objective Management Group**

Keeping it real! This book is about stopping the nonsense and George does not hold back with his upfront insights on the biggest issues sales teams are struggling with. Read it, apply it and you too will stop killing deals.

- **Mark Hunter, The Sales Hunter**

Wide-ranging content in a lean, tight package from one of today's clearest sales thinkers. George sets out the problem—a mix of human behaviors that interfere with sales success plus ingrained sales myths and tech systems that exacerbate the problems. Then he lays out simple, logical steps toward a solution that any sales leader and team can follow. A brilliant book!

- **Barbara Weaver Smith, Founder & CEO, The Whale Hunters**

CONTENTS

Foreword by Jason Jordan   9

1 A NEW VISION FOR SALES   12
Introduction   12
Assumptions that kill   15
How to get the most out of this book   16
Who the book is not for   17

2 SALESPEOPLE ARE BORN, NOT MADE, RIGHT?   18
Humans are illogical creatures   18
Limiting beliefs are limiting   19
"Salespeople are born" is a limiting belief   22
How this belief kills deals   26
Why performance must be cultivated   27

3 SHOULDN'T SALESPEOPLE BE MORE DISCIPLINED?   33
The world's most disciplined people aren't very disciplined   34
What is self-discipline and what is willpower?   36
Willpower is depletable   38
Or is it?   46
Self-discipline in the sales organization   48

4 WHAT DRIVES BUYING AND SELLING BEHAVIOR?   50
The neuro-science of decision-making   51
Why logic doesn't drive decisions   52
Logic vs the sale   54
Five actual drivers of decisions   58

5   HOW TECHNOLOGY UNDERMINES SALES   68

A brief history of the CRM   69
How technology undermines sales   74
The state of sales technology   78

6   STOP THE BLEEDING   82

How one surgeon stopped thousands of deaths   83
His secret: checklists and reinforcement   85
How to stop deals from dying, too   86

7   HEAL THE ORGANIZATION   96

What is sales enablement?   97
Assess your team and environment   98
Prioritize, reinforce, integrate   105
From strategy to process, to skills development   106
Embedding learning into workflows   108
Make it beautiful!   111

8   ACHIEVE WORLD-CLASS PERFORMANCE   112

How not to coach   113
What coaching should be   117
How to build an effective coaching structure   119

9   MAKE YOUR TECHNOLOGY THE SERVANT OF YOUR PEOPLE   134

Tech should enable your unique way of selling   134
The tech problem   135
The Siren song of AI   137
How to make your machines the servant,
not the master   139

0   ACKNOWLEDGMENTS   150

About George Brontén   152

FOREWORD

As I've made my way through a long and varied career in sales, I've observed that there are at least four types of people in sales forces.

First, there are the folks who shun any type of rigor or discipline. These are the gunslinging soloists who intend to succeed based on their innate skill or personality. To these performance artists, there is nothing more offensive than the notion of adhering to a rigid sales process. Sales processes feel like heavy weights strapped to their ankles, slowing them to a crawl. These people succeed or fail on their own merits—often very quickly.

Then there are the salespeople who are attracted to discipline. They like that there are best practices in sales, and they work to learn and perfect them. They gladly use processes, technology, and other sales enablers. They like sales training, and they like to be coached. And throughout their careers, their capability and performance steadily improve as they deliberately add to their skillset. They are solid performers and the backbone of any professional sales force.

Next are the innovators. These are the sellers and sales leaders who have mastered the best practices and strive to improve them. They constantly tinker with the processes and technology in order to make them more efficient and effective. They push high-flying sales forces even higher through an obsession with observation, measurement, and continuous improvement. Perhaps they end up at the top of the sales org chart, or perhaps they find their way into sales operations or consulting. They are the experts in all things sales.

Then there are the rarest of creatures in sales: the people who for whatever reason have a transcendent vision. Of course they understand the processes, the technology, the coaching, the metrics—but they view them from the outside, not from within. They see them as pieces of a larger mosaic, and they judge them with critical eyes. They appreciate both the beauty and the absurdity of how sales forces operate, and they are deft at putting things into perspective. They are the thought leaders who ultimately push the profession forward.

When I first encountered George Bróntén, I suspected he was one of these rarities. I found his writing to be insightful and his ideas refreshing. When I later met him, I thoroughly enjoyed our conversation and looked forward to the next. Since then I've come to know him as a true thought leader and a genuinely good guy. George is the kind of person who could write a book that would make seasoned sales professionals stop and think. And now he has done just that.

The book you hold in your hands is unlike most before it. It is not a deep dive into sales methodology or technique; rather, it's a guided journey to the outside of sales, and then a discerning look back in. It's a holistic view of the mosaic, from behavior to psychology, from process to mythology, from enablement to technology. It puts everything in its place, pointing out the flaws in modern sales forces. But most importantly, it addresses not only the tools of the sales force, but also the humanity. Sales forces are, after all, a collection of salespeople—an obvious fact that is typically overlooked in sales management frameworks. Not overlooked here.

I won't preview the content of the book because George has woven the story line carefully. But I will say to prepare yourself for something out of the ordinary. I don't think I have ever seen someone pull such varied subject matter into a book on sales, but it works. It works wonderfully, actually, to point out the flawed assumptions that torture most sales forces and the new perspective that's required to end the suffering. Read this book carefully, and read it again. Then you can stamp out those bad assumptions, build a new way of selling, and stop killing deals!

— **Jason Jordan**
Author, *Cracking the Sales Management Code*

1

A NEW VISION FOR SALES

WHAT THIS BOOK IS ABOUT

This is not a traditional book. It is a map of the unconscious assumptions that impact sales, a practical tool for driving world-class sales performance, and a new vision for the future of sales organizations.

I created it for leaders who want to massively improve sales performance in a complex b2b environment. For people who are willing to look below the surface and question their assumptions to find the roots of problems and the source of solutions. For leaders who are willing to take a deep dive into the subconscious and face the demons that undermine organizational performance. For brave individuals willing to take on those demons, defeat them, and build a whole new vision and structure for their sales organizations.

THE STORY OF THIS BOOK STARTS WITH MY STORY.

In 2009, the company I had built was losing money, hundreds of thousands of dollars at a time, with nothing to show for it.

The problem continued month after month, year after year, and I couldn't make it stop.

To understand the root of the problem, we have to go back to 1998 in Stockholm. My company at that time, Upstream, was in the business of finding little-known pieces of software and selling them through a network of IT resellers.

The business was transactional, with profits based on volume, and I was a sales team of one.

We enjoyed some success with the model, but we wanted to do even bigger things. We visited 350 of our resellers and had a deep-dive conversation about how they were doing and what challenges they were facing.

Out of those conversations, we identified a problem we could solve using software. We designed a business model that helped our resellers convert their low-profit organizations into businesses with 20 to 30 percent profit margins.

The customers of the new business loved us. Deliverables were scalable with high margins. It seemed as if we were on the right track. But this is also where our troubles began.

MY OWN BUSINESS MODEL HAD SHIFTED, IN TWO KEY WAYS:

1. **Our b2b sales** environment had moved from high-volume transactional to complex.
2. **Our sales organization** needed to scale up in order for our business to scale up.

Our new offering was both high risk and intrusive—two marks of a complex b2b sale—and required skilled and high-touch interactions with each potential customer. I had brought my brother in as a salesperson, and as long as my brother and I were the only salespeople, this wasn't a problem. We understood our product and the needs of our customers intimately, and we both know how to sell. Side by side, we grew the business and improved our margins.

But then we recruited our first professional salesperson.

Then fired our first salesperson.
Then hired our second.
And fired our second.
And hired.
And fired.
And hired.
And fired.

And each time we spent tens of thousands of dollars in recruitment fees, onboarding and training, in addition to the costs of salary, benefits, and severance. Each time the process cost us about $100,000, plus a lot of killed deals. It hurt.

Our sales organization was in critical condition.

At first, I blamed the people we were hiring—and the recruiters. But as is usually the case when something is troubling me, the real problem was me.

The roots of poor performance, in sales or anything else, are

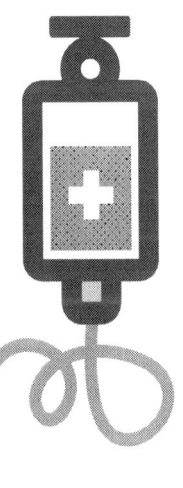

never "out there." It is not the technology, the people, the system, the environment, or the product that fails us. Instead, the problem is "in here"— in the subconscious assumptions we make, which have very real, very practical consequences "out there" in the world of money and relationships.

> YOUR ASSUMPTIONS ARE YOUR WINDOWS ON THE WORLD. SCRUB THEM OFF EVERY ONCE IN A WHILE, OR THE LIGHT WON'T COME IN.
> ~ ISAAC ASIMOV

This book will take you on a journey through the subconscious to meet the three main bad assumptions (our unconscious "demons") that impact sales performance. Then it will unveil for you a fresh, truly effective framework for defeating those demons and developing a world-class, customer-focused sales organization.

The concepts, ideas, and framework in this book are built on research across a broad range of nonsales disciplines, alongside insights and research gleaned from experts in our industry, and supplemented by my own personal experience.

The framework presented in these pages and supplemental materials will help you differentiate your organization by how you sell, so you can easily and consistently outcompete your peers. And it will do so while showing you how to consistently and systematically treat customers and team members like the valuable humans that they are.

HOW TO USE THIS BOOK

To make this book as useful and valuable as possible, I have kept it simple and focused on the key points. Then, to help you implement the concepts presented here, I've created an online resource center, which contains templates, calculators, exercises, worksheets, white papers, and other tools designed to make it easy to execute on the principles in this book.

 You can find that resource center at ***https://stop.killing.deals/resources.*** I recommend that you go ahead and bookmark the resource center now, as I'll be referring to it throughout the book.

While you're on the resource center page, go ahead and use the sales enablement ROI calculator to help you track the value of the principles in this book. By filling it out now, at the start of your journey, you'll be able to look back and see the tangible results of your inner and outer work.

Like any other tool, this book and its accompanying resources can be used in a variety of ways. You can read the book itself cover to cover and then return to each chapter individually and dive into their associated resources. You can read it one section at a time and use the resources for each chapter as you go. You can scan through it once and then use the book as a reference tool as needed.

You're also welcome to simply download the resources and start using them right away, though I do recommend that you familiarize yourself with the concepts of this book before you make drastic changes in your organization.

WHAT THIS BOOK IS NOT FOR

Before you dive in, let's be crystal clear about what you will not find in these pages.

This is not a book about high-volume, low-complexity sales.

This is not a book about sales strategy.

This is not a book about sales methodology (though it is a good companion to books about methodology).

This is not a book for those who are happy with the status quo and unmotivated to change.

This is not a book for the faint of heart.

SALESPEOPLE ARE BORN, NOT MADE, RIGHT?

As successful professionals, we like to think that we make decisions based largely on logic and reason. But science tells a different story. Social science researchers often say that most of our behavior is driven by thoughts, feelings, memories, and processes that take place below the level of our consciousness.

Many psychologists refer to this process as our unconscious. We are, by definition, unaware of what is happening in the unconscious parts of our minds, but the good news is that most of our thoughts are helpful and supportive. For instance, the actions you take to complete basic daily tasks such as making coffee, doing dishes, and turning on your computer are largely done at a level below consciousness, saving you countless time and effort on these routine tasks.

To prove this to yourself, go make yourself a sandwich. As you're doing so, think about each motion you make, from opening the refrigerator to opening the deli drawer to closing your hand around the bag of sandwich slices. Think about which muscles you use to close your fingers around the bag and open it. How much pressure do you use? Which fingers are active and which fingers are passive in this activity? Do this for the entire process until you have a completed sandwich and see how long it takes you.

In this case, thinking about each element of the process makes the process harder. When we let our unconscious mind handle the routine, however, it frees the conscious mind to focus on bigger tasks, like our next important meeting or whether we remembered to pick up the kids from school.

In addition to unconscious processes, we all also harbor an almost infinite number of unconscious beliefs, many of them self-limiting, that impact our actions. For instance, when you give your child a hug, you probably don't spend a lot of conscious effort determining whether it is a wise course of action. Most likely, you just hug them.

That's because you (probably) have a subconscious belief that says, "My child loves me and welcomes my hugs." If, instead, you have a subconscious belief that says, "I am repulsive and nobody wants to touch me," you will probably not hug anyone, even a child, easily. As a result, you will both be deprived of important human contact and suffer as a consequence, without perhaps ever knowing why.

Both supportive (my child loves me) and unsupportive (I am repulsive) beliefs can form in our subconscious minds based on personal history, childhood experiences, social conditions, adult experiences, trauma, habit, and other ways. When these beliefs are unsupportive, we call them limiting beliefs, because they limit our potential.

Limiting beliefs among sales professionals and leaders can include beliefs such as, "I don't deserve to make a lot of money," "I'm not an effective communicator," and "People don't trust me."

Most often, people are not consciously aware of their limiting beliefs, but they can often be identified by their outcomes. For instance, a belief like "People don't trust me" can make it difficult for a salesperson to build rapport. One outcome may be that the salesperson overexplains themselves constantly. This, in turn, undermines trust, which contributes to the limiting belief in an unfortunate and damaging cycle.

Limiting beliefs can also exist at organizational and cultural levels and impact more than just one person at a time.

For instance, as a culture, we Swedes have what I consider a supportive belief that we deserve to take breaks. As a result, they are almost notorious for long, relaxing summer vacations (be jealous). By contrast, the culture in the US tends to hold the (to my mind, limiting) belief that vacation is a luxury for the wealthy and accomplished and/or to be earned only by long, hard work. As a result, Americans take far fewer, shorter, and less relaxing vacations.

FIG 1.01 Differences in beliefs change vacationing habits.

The sales industry and sales organizations also have unconsciously held beliefs and biases that drive their structure and functioning. Some of those beliefs are supportive, and some are not. Among the unsupportive beliefs, I have identified three big bad dealers of death, the bad unconscious assumptions that prevent us from making the gains in effectiveness we work so hard for, which we will look at carefully in this chapter.

These assumptions also qualify as limiting beliefs because they lead to behaviors and structures that limit your team's success.

These bad assumptions are present to some degree in almost every organization. If your sales team is highly successful already, there's a good chance that your organization holds fewer of these bad assumptions, or holds them less tightly. If your organization is struggling, on the other hand, the odds are good that you will find all of these assumptions embedded deeply in your organization's unconscious.

The good news is that unconscious beliefs and patterns can be reprogrammed at the individual, organizational, and cultural level. That's what this book is fundamentally about, and this chapter marks the start of that process.

Your first step: Make the unconscious conscious.

This and the next two chapters each unmask one of the three bad assumptions and show you how to identify such assumptions in your organization so you can begin to uproot them.

THE THREE BAD ASSUMPTIONS ARE THESE:

- Salespeople are born, not made.
- Salespeople are disciplined.
- Buyers and sellers are logical.

Let's start with the bad assumption that salespeople are born, not made.

BAD ASSUMPTION: SALESPEOPLE ARE BORN, NOT MADE

Selling is a mystical, magical talent. You're either born with it coursing through your body, you beautiful, golden-tongued, boundlessly energetic money-making creature—or you're not.

Full stop.

It sounds ridiculous when it's said this way, and you probably know better on a conscious level. But does your organization know how ridiculous this is? And are you still operating as though this terrible assumption were true? Many do, without realizing it.

In its worst manifestation, this assumption leads to the following scenario:

You hire salespeople, give them a stack of information about their products, assign them a set of goals and quotas, and set them loose with a list of cold prospects. If they're born salespeople, they make it. If they're not, they quit and you hire someone else and put them through the same trial by fire.

In less extreme conditions, your organization may provide training, management, and a rewards structure designed to motivate salespeople to try harder, but your company may not be benefiting from these structures and incentives as much as you should be.

HOW THE SALESPEOPLE-ARE-BORN-NOT-MADE ASSUMPTION KILLS SALES

You can identify the presence of the salespeople-are-born-not-made assumption in your organization by the presence of one or more of the following symptoms.

1. UNRELIABLE BUSINESS RESULTS AND SLOW OR NONEXISTENT GROWTH

If your organization believes that salespeople are born, not made, they may assign sales goals to the sales team without providing the leadership and enablement to achieve them. This leads to a sink-or-swim culture that hinders progress and undermines effectiveness while simultaneously creating an expensive and wasteful hire-and-fire cycle.

In response to missed revenue numbers, which occurs because of the lack of supportive structure, organizational leadership may increase goals to compensate. This leads to the sales organization doing more of the same unsuccessful action, but at a more frantic pace.

In this environment, many sales organizations will also experience the following:

- Excessive salesperson turnover. Salespeople who don't thrive in the sink-or-swim environment will either leave or be fired, and among them may be many people who could have been valuable team members with the right support.

- Fast sales leadership turnover. When sales leadership doesn't deliver strong business results, business leadership makes the same mistake that's being made lower down in the organization: They hire and fire, looking for a rock star manager who can perform despite suboptimal conditions.

- Missed forecasts. The same problems that make it impossible to deliver consistently on business results make it impossible to accurately predict them.

- Unhappy stakeholders. In this volatile environment, investors and other stakeholders get restless. You may see high turnover in other parts of the organization and unpleasant pressure from investors.

2. A NEEDLESSLY STRESSFUL WORK ENVIRONMENT

It's a common misconception that sales is always a high-stress job. While it can be challenging to meet high expectations, a healthy sales organization should feel vibrant and alive, not stressful and frantic. Salespeople should feel empowered to meet their goals, not panicky that they may not.

In a needlessly stressful environment, salespeople who perform well by gut may internalize the idea that they're simply better than others and may hoard information and knowledge to maintain that illusion. They may be more likely to resist training and new processes because of the mistaken idea that the reason they're so successful is that they were born this way and should just be left to their own devices.

Some high performers will leave for opportunities with organizations that provide more support and less stress.

Meanwhile, salespeople who are struggling may internalize the idea that they are failures and either quit the profession altogether or go to another company.

In this environment, even high-performing salespeople won't perform at the top of their game. They may do well by comparison, but they also may miss opportunities, alienate potentially good customers, hog opportunities, and hoard information that would be more effective when shared.

3. BRAIN DRAIN AND THE LOSS OF ORGANIZATIONAL KNOWLEDGE

When we assume that salespeople are born not made, we fail to capture what it is that successful salespeople actually do that makes them successful.

Salespeople who succeed may think there's no way to share the magic with others—or they simply prefer not to.

Salespeople who struggle don't know what they don't know and don't know that they could do better with the right guidance.

Meanwhile, the organization could be benefiting from the capture, retention, and propagation of sales knowledge and skills practiced by its top salespeople. But instead, that knowledge exists only in the instincts of select salespeople and is lost completely when those people move on to another company or into retirement.

Treating sales as a born-not-made profession prevents your organization from developing a true way of selling that is consistent and effective across the organization. Instead of viewing your way of selling as valuable intellectual capital, which can be molded for competitive advantage, you may be letting it walk right out your door every time a senior salesperson leaves.

WHY YOUR TOP PERFORMERS MUST BE CULTIVATED, NOT PLUCKED FULLY MATURE FROM THE WILD

Wouldn't it be nice if you could walk out your front door and pluck delicious, fully cooked meals, tailored to your dietary requirements, straight off a tree that just happened to grow there?

We all know this is not possible, yet we treat the sales profession as if it ought to work this way. Just like a tree can't grow to your specifications without cultivation, salespeople can't perform their best without something more than a stack of product info and a prospect list. Why?

FIG 1.02 You can't expect to pluck top sales performers from trees.

1. SELLING IS DIFFERENT IN DIFFERENT ENVIRONMENTS

Even if your new salesperson was highly successful at a former company, you can't assume they will automatically perform well in your organization. Why? Because not all selling is created equal.

> SALES IS NOT ART. IT'S A PROFESSION THAT CAN BE ARTFULLY EXECUTED.
>
> ~ GEORGE BRONTÉN

Some specifics of your sales environment may be similar to those of other organizations, such as your industry, offerings, and market.

Others will be mostly or completely unique: Your positioning, messaging, strategy, methodology, and sales process, for instance.

In addition, the complexity of your sales environment will fall somewhere along a continuum, which means it isn't likely to match the complexity of the salesperson's former training and experience.

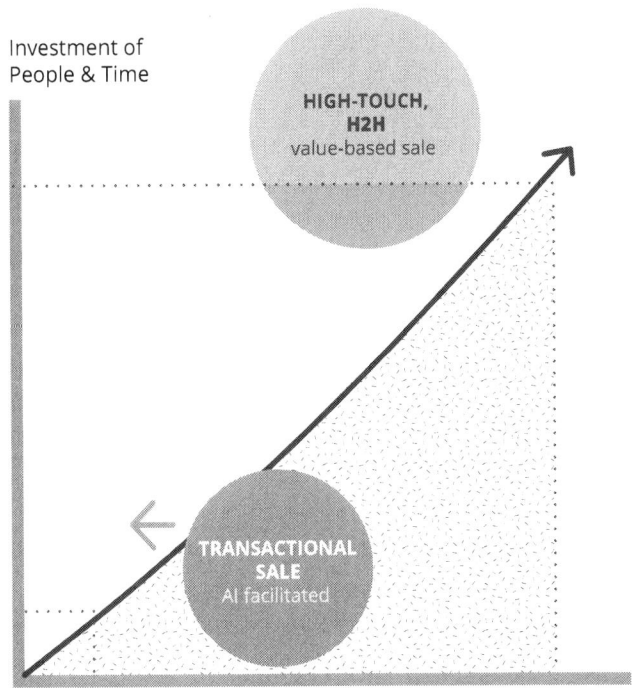

Investment of
People & Time

**HIGH-TOUCH,
H2H**
value-based sale

**TRANSACTIONAL
SALE**
AI facilitated

Perceived risk for buyer

FIG 1.03 The sales complexity continuum: Sales complexity operates along a continuum based on two key factors: How the buyer perceives their risk and the intrusiveness of your solution. (Graphic inspired by the work of Prosales Institute.)

Cost is often considered a primary factor in whether a sale is considered complex, but the reality is that cost is only one factor impacting the buyer's perception of the investment's risk, and perceived risk is a better measure for complexity. Buyer's perception of risk can be impacted by these factors:

- How much money and time the buyer invests in the purchasing process

- How much money and time the buyer will invest in implementation
- The number of people involved in the purchase and implementation
- Whether the decision is tied to key business initiatives
- The cost of potential failure to the company and individuals' careers
- The buyer's personal sensitivity to risk

Intrusiveness relates to how much the purchase will interact with and disrupt the buyer's current way of doing things. It increases according to a number of factors, including these:

- Need to change business processes, workflows, and behaviors
- Number of interactions your solution will have with other business units and tools
- Number of integrations with buyer's technology
- Number of people involved in the implementation
- Length of implementation, taking people away from their daily commitments
- How and in what ways the purchase will impact operations, customer service, and support

The higher the perceived risk and intrusiveness of the offering, the more complex the sale will be. At the low-complexity end of the scale, a transactional, automated sales environment may make salespeople more or less interchangeable and require minimal training. At the high-complexity end of the scale, salespeople need significant and detailed skills, enablement, and coaching in order to succeed.

Within the spectrum of complexity is an enormous amount of variation up and down both sides of the scale and along all of the possible additional axes. How many stakeholders are involved, alignment with key initiatives, the internal political landscape, how many departments will be affected, technical difficulties, pricing model, competitive environment, and many more factors will impact how selling must take place.

INVESTMENT
of people & time

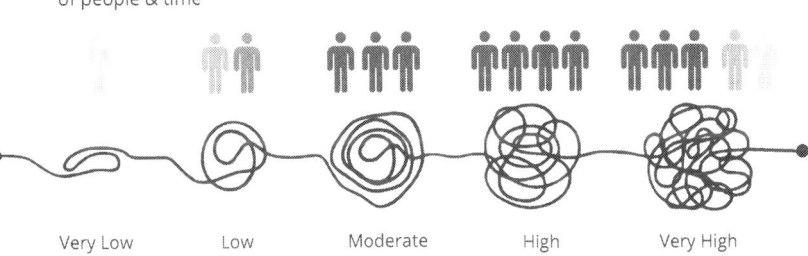

Very Low   Low   Moderate   High   Very High

FIG 1.04 Sales complexity is highly influenced by the number of people involved.

2. THE SELLING ENVIRONMENT CHANGES CONSTANTLY

Gone are the days of Rolodexes and analog telephones. Today's selling environment is not only more complex, it is also faster paced and changing more quickly than ever before.

New technologies, new approaches, new competitors, and new insights seem to crop up overnight.

Meanwhile, customer behavior shifts almost as quickly. Globalization and the rise of content marketing has shifted how and where buyers get their information. Larger buying committees and shifts in who makes buying decisions mean that the b2b environment must constantly adapt.

> SALES PROFESSION-
> ALS HAVE TO LEARN,
> UNLEARN, AND RELEARN
> VERY QUICKLY DUE TO
> RAPIDLY CHANGING
> BUYING ENVIRONMENTS.
>
> **~ TAMARA SCHENK**
> SALES ENABLEMENT EVANGE-
> LIST, ANALYST, ADVISOR, AND
> SPEAKER

3. GREAT SALESPEOPLE ALSO GET BETTER WITH ENABLEMENT

Maybe you've managed to assemble a team of superheroes, salespeople who perform no matter what, who go out and get 'em and close deals in any environment, in any conditions, despite everything.

CONGRATULATIONS.

You're still going to be outcompeted by organizations that have figured out how to attract high performers and also enable them to even higher performance.

3

SALESPEOPLE ARE DISCIPLINED
(NO, THEY AREN'T)

"My salespeople know what to do, but they just won't do it consistently."

If you've ever issued this complaint, you have been a victim of a second bad assumption: Salespeople are disciplined.

You may think, "I know they're not disciplined, but they should be." For our purposes, these assumptions are essentially the same, and they are both wrong.

Unlike the previous bad assumption (salespeople are born, not made), you may actually believe this assumption consciously as well as subconsciously. You look at your sales team and see that some of them are doing everything they're supposed to do, and some are not. You look at your daily habits and see that you are mostly consistent in doing the right things, and it's easy to be frustrated by the fact that not everyone on your team is.

Despite this apparent evidence that self-discipline is simply something salespeople should be exercising more of, science tells us otherwise. According to current neuropsychology research, the truth is that we humans naturally have a limited capacity for discipline.

To demonstrate the reality of this assumption, let's take a look at discipline among some of the world's most disciplined people: Surgeons.

HOW EVEN THE WORLD'S MOST DISCIPLINED PEOPLE AREN'T AS DISCIPLINED AS THEY SHOULD BE

Surgeons might be considered among the world's most disciplined people. It takes a lot of discipline to make it through the decades of education, training, and internship required to practice medicine and to maintain credentials and compliance, all while meeting hospital regulations and taking care of patient needs.

Yet, there is substantial evidence that surgeons are not as self-disciplined as we might like to believe. Consider the following story.

The pop artist Andy Warhol was a central figure of popular culture through most of the '60s, '70s, and '80s in the US. Most people recognize at least a few of his iconic images, such as his depictions of Marilyn Monroe and the Campbell's soup can. Many can even connect his name with them.

But fame did not insulate him from the consequences of poor discipline on his medical team. In 1987, at the age of fifty-eight, he went into surgery for his gall bladder and came out in apparently good condition. Two hours later, he was dead.

His estate contends that his death was caused by medical professionals who pumped his body full of too many fluids and didn't adequately monitor his intake and output. The result, they said, was that his body overloaded and his heart failed.

It's important to note that the hospital where he died disputes this interpretation of events. They said his medical condition was delicate and that his death was not preventable. We may never know for sure in this particular case, but it highlights a problem that is endemic in the medical profession: medically induced injuries and deaths.

An eight-year Johns Hopkins patient safety study determined that 250,000 US deaths per year are due to medical error, also known as iatrogenic injuries, making it the third leading cause of death after heart disease and cancer.

From failing to properly drape a patient for IV in-

FIG 1.05 Healthcare mistakes cause millions of deaths yearly.

sertion, to inadequate presurgical hygiene, iatrogenic injury highlights that even surgeons aren't as disciplined as they should be.

Why is this?

To answer that question, first we must establish a common understanding of the meaning of self-discipline.

WHAT IS SELF-DISCIPLINE?

One dictionary defines self-discipline as the ability to control yourself and to make yourself work hard or behave in a particular way without needing anyone else to tell you what to do.

Another word for self-discipline is willpower. According to the American Psychological Association:

> We have many common names for willpower: determination, drive, resolve, self-discipline, self-control. But psychologists characterize willpower, or self-control, in more specific ways. According to most psychological scientists, willpower can be defined as: The ability to delay gratification, resisting short-term temptations in order to meet long-term goals. The capacity to override an unwanted thought, feeling, or impulse. The ability to employ a "cool" cognitive system of behavior rather than a "hot" emotional system. Conscious, effortful regulation of the self by the self. A limited resource capable of being depleted.

Let's break this down.

Willpower is the ability to delay gratification, resisting short-term temptations in order to meet long-term goals.

In the sales profession, for instance, willpower is the ability to ask the questions that get to the heart of the matter, even when you have an impulse not to. It's to document what was said in a meeting in order to improve effectiveness in the future, instead of moving quickly on to the next opportunity for a quick gain. It means time out of the week to focus on self-improvement and training instead of doing activities that might generate some immediate revenue.

Willpower is the capacity to override an unwanted thought, feeling, or impulse.

It's the capacity to make small, daily decisions for long-term results rather than short-term gratification. It's overriding the impulse to head to the water cooler instead of immediately finding and sharing a case study to support a point you made in a sales call. It's overriding the impulse to retreat to a comfortable topic with a prospect instead of asking a challenging question that will move the sale forward. It's overriding the desire to bounce back to old behaviors instead of practicing new skills.

Willpower is the ability to employ a "cool" cognitive system of behavior rather than a "hot" emotional system.

It's responding to customers with empathy rather than anger and frustration. It's resisting the urge to offer discounts prematurely out of a sense of discomfort or fear. It's following a best-practice process rather than jumping forward too fast in response to a prospect's expressed urgency.

Willpower is a conscious, effortful regulation of the self by the self.

It takes conscious, consistent effort.

Willpower is a limited resource capable of being depleted.

Like other forms of conscious effort fueled by energy, willpower is depletable. It bears noting that this point is in dispute, as I'll discuss later. Nevertheless, let us explore the implications of this statement.

WILLPOWER CAN BE DEPLETED

You feel this to be true, even if you've never said it out loud to yourself.

Remember the last weekend you spent with difficult relatives, smiling politely even though they were getting on your very last nerve? Remember how, as soon as you could get away, you got yourself a triple-scoop deluxe chocolate heart attack sundae? Or had that huge pizza, despite being on a diet?

You used up your willpower choosing repeatedly not to give your mother-in-law a piece of your mind and resisted the urge to tell your aunt to mind her own damn business.

A huge amount of research backs up this concept of willpower.

In one early academic study, Roy Baumeister's social psychology lab brought subjects into a room filled with the aroma of freshly baked cookies. On a table was a plate of cookies and a bowl of radishes. Some of the study participants were encouraged to indulge in the cookies, while others were encouraged instead to snack on radishes.

Afterward, all subjects were given a test of willpower, involving a difficult geometric puzzle.

Can you guess which group performed better?

Those who had indulged in cookies persisted at the task

for an average of almost nineteen minutes. Those who had exercised willpower by snacking on radishes gave up after about eight minutes.

The radish-eaters used up their willpower and retained only half the willpower of their cookie-indulging peers.

Resisting indulgence isn't the only way willpower can be depleted. It's also depleted by making choices, especially difficult ones.

In another study, a Princeton University doctoral candidate named Dean Spears visited two villages in India: one richer and one poorer. His team asked participants to engage in a common test of willpower involving squeezing a handgrip. Afterward, he offered them an opportunity to purchase soap at a significant discount. Then he administered the willpower test again.

For the members of the richer community, the decision to buy the soap was easy, as it represented a tangible benefit that was easy for them to achieve without sacrifice. For members of the poorer communities, however, the purchase represented a substantial short-term sacrifice relative to their means, making the decision a difficult one with potential risks and rewards on both sides.

As predicted, participants performed more poorly on the willpower exercise after making a difficult decision than before, while those for whom the decision was easy performed almost as well the second time as the first.

There is also research to indicate that making decisions over the course of a day, even small ones, has the effect of gradually wearing down one's willpower.

Steve Jobs famously wore the same turtleneck every day to work so that he wouldn't have to make decisions about clothing early in the day that might impact his resources for bigger and more important decisions later.

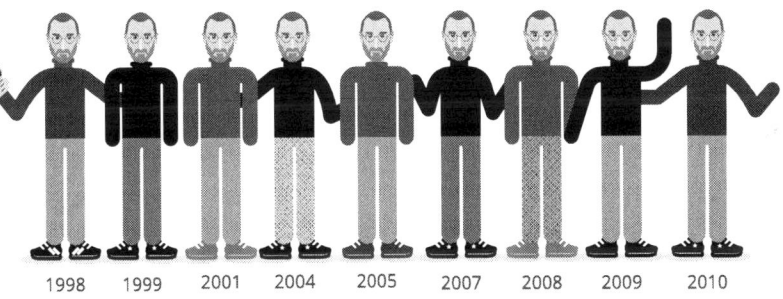

FIG 1.06 Steve Jobs famously wore a black turtleneck, blue jeans, and sneakers, every day.

BUT IS WILLPOWER ACTUALLY DEPLETABLE? OR DO WE MAKE IT SO BY BELIEVING IT SO?

So far so good. The research backs up what we have all personally experienced about willpower: It is depletable.

More recent research calls the idea into question, presenting evidence that it may be depletable only because we believe it to be depletable.

In a 2010 study by Veronika Job at Stanford University, researchers asked study participants about their beliefs. They then tested their willpower depletion. Those who said that willpower was a limited resource were more likely to have their willpower depleted than those who believed it was unlimited.

In a second part of the study, researchers asked participants to fill out a questionnaire with subtly biased questions that were designed to manipulate their beliefs about willpower. In this portion of the study, those who had been led to believe that willpower is a limited resource performed worse on the subsequent willpower exercise than those who were led to believe willpower is an unlimited resource.

SO WHICH IS IT? DEPLETABLE OR NOT?

The scientific research is still inconclusive about the exact nature of willpower, but there is no question that most people experience willpower as depletable. The important takeaway for sales organizations is that we must start from the assumption that our salespeople are not going to exercise unlimited willpower unless we support them more effectively.

Fortunately, additional research into the nature of willpower has yielded some promising leads on how to do that. Here are two useful facts the research shows about willpower:

- Willpower can be conserved.
- Willpower can be strengthened.

WILLPOWER CAN BE CONSERVED

A classic study from the 1970s by Walter Mischel, a psychologist while at Stanford, used marshmallows to test the willpower of children. In the study, children were offered a marshmallow and told that they could either eat it, or they could wait an unspecified amount of time and then they would get two marshmallows.

The researchers placed the marshmallow on the table in front of the children and left the room.

They made a note of which children ate the marshmallows and which children waited for the researcher to return with the second marshmallow, and then compared that information against the performance of the children later in life on measures such as educational attainment, body mass index, and SAT scores.

The study famously concluded that children who exercised self-discipline and the ability to delay gratification performed better on average on standard life success measures.

FIG 1.07 The faces of indecision among children in Mischel's famous marshmallow study of willpower.

Clearly, self-discipline has many benefits. But that's not the only trait the study revealed. It also revealed specific tactics that enabled the successful children to sustain their self-discipline—tactics such as closing their eyes, looking away from the marshmallow, or otherwise distracting themselves.

This study implies that avoiding temptation can allow people to conserve their willpower and reinforces the idea that there may be other ways as well, including Steve Jobs's famous approach to make fewer unimportant decisions (wear the same thing every day).

WILLPOWER CAN BE STRENGTHENED

A study by psychologist Mark Muraven at the University at Albany was one of the first to demonstrate that willpower can be strengthened. Researchers asked participants to follow a two-week regimen that required self-discipline, including tracking their food intake, moods, and posture.

When compared to a control group that did not specifically practice self-discipline during the two weeks, participants who exercised their self-discipline performed better on subsequent tests of willpower and were less likely to have depleted willpower.

HOW TO IDENTIFY THE SELF-DISCIPLINE ASSUMPTION LURKING INSIDE YOUR ORGANIZATION

There's a good chance that you already know you've been operating under the bad assumption that salespeople are naturally disciplined. But even if you know better now, there are probably symptoms indicating that this bad assumption still lurks below the level of consciousness within your organization.

Some of those symptoms lie in the questions you and your fellow sales leaders ask:

- Why won't my salespeople comply with reporting?
- Why won't they use the technologies we buy for them?
- Why won't they follow the process steps?
- Why won't they apply their new skills?
- Why do they quit trying after they meet quota?
- Why won't they have hard conversations?
- Why don't they invite more stakeholders to meetings?

Organizationally, the symptoms may look like this:

- Unreliable sales forecasts
- Low quota attainment
- Less-than-impressive win rates
- Undisciplined discounting
- Slow ramp-up times for new hires

APPLY A CORRECT UNDERSTANDING OF DISCIPLINE INSIDE THE SALES ORGANIZATION

Knowing that this bad assumption lurks in your organization is the first step to uprooting it. Instead of blaming salespeople, you can begin supporting them. Some of the actions you can take include:

- Reducing the amount of willpower required to complete daily tasks
- Reducing the number of unimportant decisions salespeople need to make on a daily basis
- Reducing the difficulty of decisions that are necessary
- Systematically reinforcing activities that steadily strengthen willpower over time
- Encouraging a mindset of willpower strength and nondepletion

All of these approaches will be addressed in more detail in later chapters when I discuss the frameworks for more effective sales organizations. But before we proceed, let's address another layer in the issue of discipline: organizational discipline.

THE PROBLEM OF ORGANIZATIONAL DISCIPLINE

One of the ironies of the industry is that we love to complain about salesperson discipline (and lack thereof), but we really hate to look at the fact that we, as an industry, and we, as organizations, usually lack discipline ourselves.

At the root of this problem is the fact that sales as a profession hasn't been taken seriously for most of its history. There is a public perception that it's dirty and sleazy and not worthy of serious study. There's an internal perception that it's an art form and that you either have it or you don't (see Chapter Two on the bad assumption that salespeople are born, not made).

The result is that the body of serious research into sales is limited, while rigorous academic study of the subject is still rare. Historically, most research belongs to for-profit entities that have a vested interest in holding the research close to their vests and/or selling it to only those who can afford it, and some organizations design and interpret studies mainly to sell their services.

This lack of academic and industry discipline reflects itself in our lack of organizational discipline. Few sales organizations maintain a clear and up-to-date strategy that is executed through a formal and dynamic process. Even fewer execute on that process with clearly defined milestones and steps and methodology.

And among those elite few, even fewer have the technological resources to effectively reinforce and enable their process. From that even smaller subset, yet even fewer collect data about sales and analyze it in an effective, systematic manner aimed at coaching behaviors and optimizing how salespeople sell.

In short, we expect individual salespeople to do what we as organizations and as an industry are not doing: establish and maintain sensible discipline.

The good news is that the answer to both problems is the same. Recognize the bad assumption, uproot it, and establish organizational discipline that supports individual discipline. In the last four chapters of this book, I'll present the framework for accomplishing exactly this.

> THERE IS ONE PLACE THAT SALES HAS WOEFULLY TRAILED OTHER BUSINESS DISCIPLINES: DISCIPLINE ITSELF.
>
> ~JASON JORDAN
> AUTHOR, *CRACKING THE SALES MANAGEMENT CODE*

4 BUYERS AND SELLERS ARE LOGICAL (NOT REALLY)

Most of us operate on a daily basis as though we and the people around us are or at least should be logical decision-making creatures.

In the sales industry, for instance, we may focus on developing messages and sales processes that will convince buyers to buy our products and services based on features and benefits. We train our salespeople and expect them to do the tasks we tell them to do because they make sense, without addressing the nonlogical reasons they may not choose to do them.

By now, however, you are beginning to understand the bad assumption (our third) that people are logical creatures. That statement isn't as true as we wish it were.

You know people are often not logical because you've seen it yourself: Buyers and sellers often make decisions and behave in ways that simply don't make sense.

Yet we continue to behave as though people are, or ought to be, logical—and it's one of the deadliest mistakes we make.

In this chapter, we'll go deep into the neuroscience of decision-making and take a look at how nonlogical decision-making behavior impacts both buyers and sellers.

THE NEUROSCIENCE OF DECISION-MAKING BEHAVIOR

In his groundbreaking work, *Thinking, Fast and Slow*, author Daniel Kahneman explains that logic is much harder work than we realize. And because it is such hard work and we are not as disciplined as we think we are, humans don't often engage in true rational thinking.

Instead, he says, we rely on a series of thinking shortcuts to get us through the day, while reserving our true logical thinking for high-priority activities and important decisions. This idea was illustrated in the sandwich-making exercise I suggested in Chapter Two.

Unfortunately, our unconscious mental shortcuts sometimes misfire, leading us to illogical conclusions. Worse, because the process takes place mostly at a subconscious level, these bad decisions *feel* logical to us, even though they often lead to poor outcomes.

In addition, the decisions we make, which generally feel like logical or at least mentally chosen decisions, are not—and cannot be—made logically.

THE ROLE OF EMOTION IN DECISION-MAKING

Neuroscientist Antonio Damasio, author of *Descartes' Error* and chair in neuroscience at the University of Southern California, is well known for his work with patients who suffered from specific types of brain injuries.

His most famous case involves Elliot (not his real name) who was an accomplished businessperson with a happy family life until a brain tumor damaged part of his frontal lobe.

Elliot had undergone a seemingly successful surgery to remove the tumor. After the surgery, he retained all of his previous skills, knowledge, intelligence, and use of his body. Doctors proclaimed it a complete recovery.

But shortly thereafter, Elliot's life fell completely apart for no apparent reason. He went through a divorce. Remarried. Divorced again. He lost his job. He got another one and lost it too. He got involved with a con artist, filed bankruptcy, and went to live with his brother.

One of Damasio's early observations was that Elliot was not only intelligent and skilled, he was thoughtful and careful in his analysis of options. In fact, he kept thousands of lists, charts, diagrams, and files full of information, plans, and analysis regarding every decision he needed to make.

What he didn't seem able to do, however, was execute on any of those plans. He had all of the material and logical capacity for decision-making but seemed nevertheless incapable of actually making those decisions.

A secondary, and seemingly unrelated observation by Damasio, was that Elliot spoke about his life as though it were someone else's, as if he were an impartial observer. He showed no apparent emotion, even about the loss of his marriage or the currently dysfunctional quality of his life.

Based on this second observation, Damasio administered a battery of tests designed to examine a person's response to emotionally charged images, such as gruesome accidents, burning buildings, and dying people.

Elliot demonstrated no emotional response.

Damasio hypothesized that Elliot's tumor or surgery damaged or removed a portion of the brain responsible for generating emotion. Furthermore, he suggested, the lack of emotional attachment was at the root of Elliot's apparent inability to make decisions. He took this hypothesis to the medical community and collected case studies and additional research. The collected evidence made it quite clear: Without the capacity for emotion, a person cannot make decisions.

Later research uncovered the reason for the correlation between emotion and decisions: Logic can be used to identify, analyze, and sort options, but not to rank them. Logic alone creates a situation so full of options and information that we become paralyzed. In a healthy brain, we use our emotions to rank options and choose the path forward. Feelings allow us to cut through the noise and choose one.

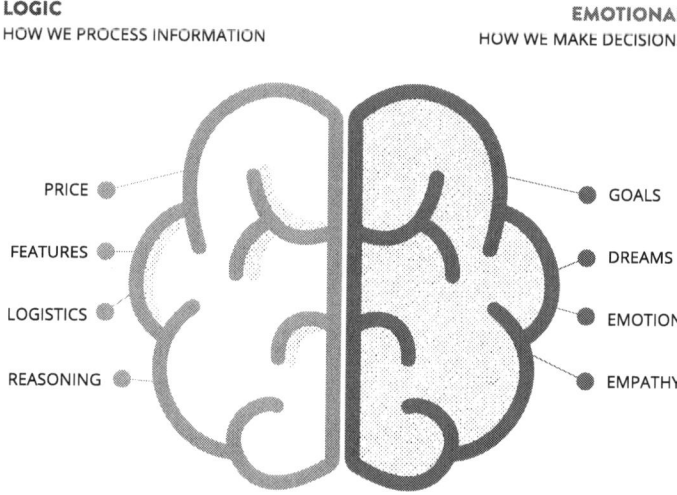

LOGIC
HOW WE PROCESS INFORMATION

EMOTIONAL
HOW WE MAKE DECISIONS

PRICE

FEATURES

LOGISTICS

REASONING

GOALS

DREAMS

EMOTION

EMPATHY

FIG 1.08 Both logic and emotion are needed to make good decisions.

HOW DOES ASSUMING PEOPLE ARE LOGICAL KILL DEALS?

Imagine your sales team in a conference room presenting a solution to potential clients. The buying team seems engaged, and your solution is a perfect logical fit to their need, but the sale doesn't go through.

Often, this scenario occurs because of what is going on under the surface, in the nonlogical murk of each buyer's subconscious.

For instance, Rebecca, the VP, is new to her administrative role. She's feeling tense because so much is changing under her feet. She doesn't realize this is why she feels antagonistic to your solution, but the reality is, she just doesn't want to handle more change right now, and that emotion ultimately dictates her decision.

One of their technical experts, Matt, regularly plays online games and uses social media, two activities that provide steady "hits" of the natural hormones dopamine and cortisol. Over time, Matt has become addicted to these hormones. His need for fresh hits means that he's checking his phone notifications under the table while your technical expert speaks. As a result of Matt's disengagement, he's not asking the detailed technical questions that would help the buying team understand the superiority of your solution, and ultimately they feel more comfortable sticking with what they've already got.

There's Francis, the CEO. She looks as if she's listening, but she's silently annoyed because of a mismatch in communication styles. She's a high D on the DiSC® profile, and your presenter is a high I ("DiSC" stands for Dominance, Influence, Steadiness, and Conscientiousness; continue reading for more information on DiSC profiles in sales). That's why she's waiting impatiently, tapping her foot under the table, for your team to get to the darn point, while your presenter is cheerfully recounting a story they hope will solidify the buyers' understanding of the solution. Francis isn't even aware of why she feels irritable and may pretend to be paying attention while her emotions are pointing at a solid no.

Meanwhile, the director of operations, Frank, is thinking about the money he's already spent on another consultant for the project. Even though that consultant has failed to yield results and your solution is much more promising, he hates the idea of throwing away all that money by switching to a new provider and starting over. He's not even really aware of why he doesn't want to switch consultants, but it just feels like a bad idea to him.

And then at the end of the conference table sit William and Chris, their two technical subject matter experts. Will and Chris are shooting each other eye rolls because they feel threatened by your solution. They fear it may make their jobs obsolete. Although the solution is logically better for the organization (and they know it), they experience it as wrong for them personally, and instead of listening for how the solution can help, they're listening to find reasons to convince the decision-makers not to choose you. They're not fully aware that they feel threatened, only that they don't like your solution and that they have found a lot of reasons not to like it.

Meanwhile, your sales team is operating with its own unconscious beliefs, emotions, and processes that limit their ability to compassionately and effectively respond to the buying team's nonlogical needs.

Have you experienced such a meeting? When the sales team doesn't seem to be connecting to the buyers? This scenario is an example of how subconscious emotion can drive a negative sales outcome. Each person around the table from

Rebecca to Francis to the tech people represents a different driver that impacts emotion, which your team may be completely unaware of. However, by understanding these drivers and their impact on emotions, your team can begin to work with instead of against them.

FIVE MAJOR UNCONSCIOUS DRIVERS THAT IMPACT DECISION-MAKING EMOTIONS

More potentially deal-killing monsters lurk in a person's subconscious than I can cover in a single book. Here, however, are the five that are understood to make the biggest impact on decision-making emotions on a regular basis:

1. PEOPLE HATE CHANGE

It's basic human nature to be afraid of the unknown. The unknown is what's lurking under your bed, around the corner, or hiding in your basement. Horror writers have known for centuries that the scariest monster is the one we haven't seen yet.

Change always involves the unknown. Buying involves change. And this means buying will always be scary. However, certain factors can make change more or less unpleasant, based on the context and the individual. A few things that make buyers more resistant to change:

- Environmental stress. When buyers are already overwhelmed by their environment, they'll be less open to change. For example, when they're new to their job or their organization is undergoing major strategic shifts, buyers may be too stressed to choose additional changes.
- Intrusiveness of the change. Some changes are easy, like a new phone or a pair of shoes. Some, like an Enterprise Resource Planning (ERP) system or a cross-country move, impact many layers and aspects of the buyer's life and/or work. The latter are scarier.

- Level of perceived risk. A high ticket price, long-term commitments, legal or reputational exposure, and other factors can cause the change to feel high risk.

- Individual style. Some individuals are simply more resistant to change than others, and some value personal relationships more highly than rational decision-making, or vice versa.

- Buying culture. Some cultures are more resistant than others and prioritize a cautious decision-making style. For example, a well-funded start-up may have a culture of "failing fast," which encourages fast decision-making with few repercussions for mistakes. A financial services firm, on the contrary, may have a culture of choosing reliability over flexibility and may make decisions more slowly.

- Location in the buying journey. Early in a purchasing decision, excitement over opportunities can be high, overriding fear of change. But as the change becomes closer to reality, fear of change can grow.

2. PEOPLE UNCONSCIOUSLY RESPOND TO HORMONES

When it comes to being ruled by hormones, everyone knows teenagers are culprits. But they're not alone. All humans are influenced by hormonal fluctuations, which can impact mood, energy, health, reaction times, strength, and, of course, decision-making.

These hormones are especially important in decision-making:

1. Testosterone
2. Estrogen and progesterone
3. Cortisol
4. Dopamine
5. Oxytocin

Testosterone drives aggressive, risk-taking behavior. Everyone, regardless of gender, has some level of testosterone in their system. Levels fluctuate over the course of the day. A seller with high testosterone may be more aggressive with buyers and either appear more confident or more arrogant, depending on context. Buyers with high testosterone may also be either eager to make a change and take a risk, or more combative and challenging in regard to change, depending on personal perception.

Estrogen and progesterone are often poorly understood, but they too exist in everyone regardless of gender. They impact risk-aversion, sociability, and emotional awareness. Higher progesterone in relation to estrogen seems to drive faster decision-making.

Cortisol is a stress hormone as well as an excitement hormone. It can drive risk-aversion, but it can also drive eagerness to make decisions. It is most often produced in response to stress and can drive buyers and sellers either toward a decision or away, depending on context. It can also drive an urge to reach for a hit of dopamine, which is what Matt was doing when he was checking his phone in the story above.

Dopamine is the hormone responsible for many addictions, such as drug and alcohol addictions, but also including gaming, relationships, and phone addictions. Salespeople experience a hit of dopamine when they get a new qualified lead or close a sale. Buyers experience a hit of dopamine when they purchase a cute pair of shoes (on sale) or get mentioned on social media. Sadly, a dopamine high doesn't last long and can drive people to seek more and more at the cost of other aspects of their lives or work.

Oxytocin is called the relationship hormone because it is responsible for feelings of closeness, warmth, and trust. Unlike dopamine, an oxytocin high can be long-lasting and doesn't cause addiction. It is considered a prosocial hormone because it tends to drive positive social behaviors. It's also an important hormone in purchasing because high levels of oxytocin lead to feelings of security and trust, which can mitigate fear of change and other forms of risk-aversion, while encouraging faster and larger purchases.

Buyer and seller hormones can conflict during the buying cycle. Toward the end of the sales cycle, the seller will often experience high levels of oxytocin because they believe the buyer trusts them and is likely to make the purchase (plus dopamine may heighten in anticipation of the close).

The buyer, however, is likely to have higher levels of cortisol as they contemplate the imminent investment. This mismatch can mean that the seller behaves in a confident, enthusiastic, and potentially aggressive manner at exactly the moment when the buyer needs to feel that they are in control of the decision, leading to a feeling on the part of the buyer that the seller isn't on their side.

3. PEOPLE EVALUATE BASED ON COMMUNICATION STYLE

Every individual has a unique behavioral and communication style that is a combination of hard wiring and environmental and experiential factors. The DiSC profile (a model owned by the Wiley Company) represents one way of categorizing these communication styles.

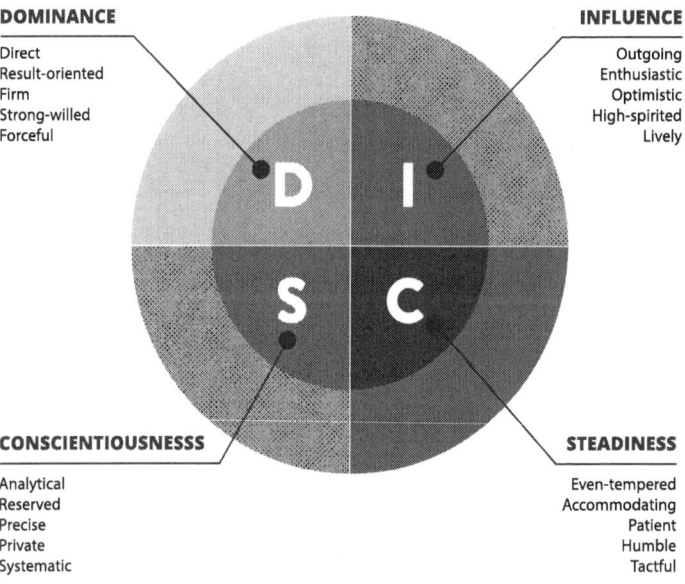

DOMINANCE

Direct
Result-oriented
Firm
Strong-willed
Forceful

INFLUENCE

Outgoing
Enthusiastic
Optimistic
High-spirited
Lively

CONSCIENTIOUSNESSS

Analytical
Reserved
Precise
Private
Systematic

STEADINESS

Even-tempered
Accommodating
Patient
Humble
Tactful

FIG 1.09 DISC: a self-assessment tool providing insight into behavioral preferences.

Using the DiSC system, you can understand buyers according to one of four profiles. C-type buyers focus on details and data for decision-making. S-type buyers focus on processes and people. I-type buyers focus on plans and success stories. D-type buyers focus on high-level solutions and getting the job done.

Regardless of which system you use for understanding different behavioral styles, when there is a mismatch, sales can go wrong. The buyer can feel uncomfortable or irritable without knowing why, which leads to objections, non-decisions, and resistance.

4. PEOPLE FALL PREY TO COGNITIVE BIAS

Cognitive bias is what happens when the mental shortcuts we use for everyday life go awry and cause us to make illogical decisions.

For instance, the sunk cost bias relates directly to our natural inclination not to agonize over every single decision every day. In general, it is safe to assume that if we have invested time or energy into something, it was worth investing time and energy into, and it makes sense to continue to do so unless there is a good reason not to.

For instance, if we have spent money renovating a house, it makes more sense to keep that house than to buy a similar house and potentially have to do similar renovations again. If we started on a project yesterday that we didn't complete, it makes sense to continue and potentially finish the project today rather than starting something else.

But in some cases, continuing to invest time and money into something we've already invested in doesn't make sense. Sellers fall prey to this all the time. You see it when they continue to pursue an old opportunity that is past its prime and unlikely to close, at the expense of new opportunities that show more promise but would require them to let go of their investment in the first opportunity.

This is also what happened to Frank, the director of operations in our conference room example. His company had already authorized substantial resources to another consultant. Even though your solution might have cost less than continuing that relationship, Frank was reluctant to make the switch.

 Thousands of cognitive biases can impact buyers and sellers. For more information about how cognitive bias affects sales, download the Cognitive Biases in Sales ebook in the resource center at *https://stop.killing.deals/resources.*

5. PEOPLE'S BEHAVIOR CAN BE DRIVEN BY LIMITING BELIEFS

At the beginning of this chapter, I mentioned how your beliefs about yourself can impact behaviors such as whether you hug your child. Likewise, your limiting beliefs about yourself can impact selling and buying behaviors.

A limiting belief is any subconscious (or conscious) belief that prevents you from getting something that you want. For instance, the belief that you are not a good speaker may prevent you from learning to present more effectively or pursue an opportunity to present at a TED conference. The belief that willpower is limited may lead you to limit your own store of willpower. And so on.

Dave Kurlan, owner of Objective Management Group, who has assessed millions of sales professionals over decades, highlights these four limiting beliefs that most often impact sales in a complex selling environment:

1. "I can't call the decision-maker."

2. "It takes a long time to get people to buy stuff."

3. "If they don't have the budget, they can't buy from me."

4. "It's not okay to talk about money and budget."

You can learn more about these limiting beliefs, their impact on sales, and how to defeat them by downloading the Limiting Beliefs in Sales white paper at *https://stop.killing.deals/resources.*

IS YOUR ORGANIZATION BEHAVING AS THOUGH SELLERS AND BUYERS ARE LOGICAL?

The assumption that people are logical is so common and diverse in its causes and impacts that it's almost certain that your organization suffers from at least some form of it.

Here are some of the possible outcomes if you buy into this bad assumption:

- Losing sales that you should have won
- Leaders throwing up their hands because they don't understand why salespeople or buyers do certain things
- Features-focused messaging instead of decision-guiding and value-focused messaging
- Sales training that ignores the human components of emotion and bias
- Expectation that if salespeople know the right thing to do, they'll just do it
- Ineffective rewards and compensation structures

Fortunately, we address this third bad assumption (that buyers and sellers are logical) the same way we address the first two bad assumptions (that salespeople are born, not made, and that salespeople are disciplined) as the first two: First, unmask the assumption wherever you find it. Then build a supportive organizational structure on a firm understanding of how humans act in the real world.

Before we move on to the framework you need to address all of the bad assumptions in your organization, we have to look at one more big problem: the fact that most sales technology is founded, built, and maintained on the premise of the three bad assumptions we just examined.

5

HOW TECHNOLOGY UNDERMINES SALES

By now, you're aware of just how much we humans don't operate like we think we do and how that impacts sales.

But the news gets worse.

What piece of technology do you rely on more than any other? Is it your CRM (customer relationship management) system? What if I told you that the entire CRM system and everything built on top of it was built on a bad foundation? What if that foundation were the three bad assumptions I outlined in the previous chapters?

What if I told you the reason you have a top-heavy, complicated, expensive technology stack is that you keep having to compensate for the way these bad assumptions affect your core technology?

That's exactly what I'm going to show you in this chapter. Here are the impacts of this unfortunate state of affairs:

- Low adoption rates
- Constant, ongoing initiatives to try to make the technology more functional
- Way too many bolted-on point solutions
- Growing complexity
- Increasing costs for all the tools and technical consultants necessary to keep the stack running

Let's examine this phenomenon by beginning at the beginning, with a brief history.

A BRIEF HISTORY OF CRM

1970s

Invented in the 1950s, the mainframe computer became more widespread for business use in the 1970s. Pioneering companies used these newly available computers in their sales and operations to digitize customer information such as names, contact details, and related data.

For sales teams, the computers provided an opportunity to digitize and share individual Rolodexes, capturing information in a central location and making it available for collaboration across the organization.

However, in order to be effective, they assumed that salespeople would logically want to share information, since it would make the organization more efficient. But since salespeople are human and therefore not purely logical, most did not share.

Some didn't because they felt (emotions) that their contact list gave them a competitive advantage against other salespeople and made them more valuable to the employer. Others didn't because they didn't want to take the time, nor did they see the value of it (discipline).

And in no case did these electronic Rolodexes teach salespeople how to be better salespeople. In the 1970s, the assumption that salespeople were born not made was even more rampant than it is today.

1980s

The 1980s marked a giant leap forward in computing technology. For the first time, computers became available in sizes small enough and cheap enough that ordinary citizens could have them in their homes. The decade also saw the advent of Microsoft Windows and a wide range of software intended for both home and business use, making the computer a practical tool for a larger number of people and companies.

In 1986, Robert and Kate Kestnbaum introduced the world's first contact management software for PCs, the precursor to the modern CRM: ACT!

ACT! collected and, to a limited degree, analyzed customer information, making it possible to digitally customize communications. ACT! had the potential to help salespeople record and access their data, and it saw better adoption rates and success than its mainframe precursors.

However, this CRM software program still struggled with the same old problem: poor adoption rates due to the assumption that salespeople are disciplined and logical. Plus, it still assumed that people either had sales in their DNA or didn't, and there was no attempt for the software to help salespeople sell better.

1990s

The 1990s saw an even wider proliferation of personal computers for both personal and business use, as well as the explosive growth of the internet and internet-based businesses. The end of the decade saw the advent of Wi-Fi and the Blackberry, further expanding the ease with which salespeople and others could access and use data and digital tools.

For marketing and sales, this decade included massive shifts in how we communicate with customers. Direct marketing via both email and snail mail became more personalized and effective. Salespeople gained access to huge amounts of information about customers that had been previously difficult to find. With the advent of Blackberry toward the end of the decade, they could even carry much of this information around with them.

Technology companies like Siebel Systems took advantage of this growth to provide a whole new generation of sales tools. They and others built on the older contact management platforms and pushed them toward sales force automation (SFA) to automate many tasks such as tracking customer interactions and inventory control.

By the end of the decade, these tools had more or less settled on the name customer relationship management (CRM) to define what they did. Many of the large CRM companies consolidated with other technology companies to integrate CRM with functions outside of the sales department, most notably to manage inventory and sales together in combined ERP and CRM systems.

While this consolidation addressed many of the organizational problems around sales and inventory, they continued to miss the mark when it came to understanding and helping the very human salespeople within the organizations they served.

In fact, the growing complexity of these systems served to reduce adoption rates even further as salespeople failed to understand how using all these technologies benefited them personally.

In response to the pressure to provide more human-friendly technologies, smaller e-CRM companies entered the market. Using the internet, intranets, and extranets, these vendors provided collaboration tools that had been unheard of previously. This is also when CRM information first became available in a handheld version via the Siebel Handheld.

Finally, famously within the software and sales space, the decade ended with the introduction of the world's first Software as a Service (SaaS) CRM called Salesforce.

At this point, CRM had become an integral and indispensable part of the sales organization and provided many useful tools with the potential to drive efficiency.

However, all of the available technologies were still operating under bad assumptions. They assumed that salespeople should know what to do and log what they've done. They were designed to make data available for use but not designed to help the humans in the organization use that data effectively.

Worse, they introduced a new problem. One that would soon plague nearly every industry that embraced new technologies during this boom and that continues to plague us today: the many-headed Hydra problem.

The problem didn't start in the sales industry, but it impacts us just the same.

THE ORIGINS AND NATURE OF THE MANY-HEADED HYDRA

"On a sunny afternoon in May, 2015, I joined a dozen other surgeons at a downtown Boston office building to begin sixteen hours of mandatory computer training." That's Atul Gawande, author of *The Checklist Manifesto*, in the New Yorker article "Why Doctors Hate Their Computers."

FIG 1.10 The many-headed hydra of technology complexity.

Gawande recounts how hopeful he felt about the new technology they were learning. He expected a steep learning curve, but then he was sure it would provide substantial benefits to the medical community.

Unfortunately, he was right about the first half and wrong about the second.

"Three years later," he said, "I've come to feel that a system that promised to increase my mastery over my work has instead increased my work's mastery over me ... Somehow we've reached a point where people in the medical profession actively, viscerally, volubly hate their computers."

How did that happen? He goes on to detail how simple technologies that were designed to solve simple problems were bolted onto other technologies designed for other problems, then expanded to solve yet more problems, and how each layer created more complexity and ended in a "massive monster of incomprehensibility."

For every problem the technology solved, it created new ones that required customizations and work-arounds, and decreased user effectiveness.

Like the mythical Hydra of ancient Greek stories, which terrorized surrounding villages and made travel impossible through its territory, for every head struck off, two new ones arose.

Unfortunately, the problem did not remain within the medical industry. In fact, it spread to almost every industry in the world. For instance—

HOW THE HYDRA COST ONE COMPANY $500 MILLION

When Lidl, a major German grocery retailer, launched a massive Enterprise Resource Planning (ERP) integration, it was supposed to make everything simpler. It would unify their inventory system and help them track their supplies and sales more effectively across their thousands of global locations.

But as the project continued, it began to show signs of stress. Each time a new function was added or a new region integrated into the system, the system's complexity grew like the head of the Hydra. And each time that happened, new code was written and new systems were implemented to solve the problems that arose. And each new layer created new complexity.

$500 million and seven years later, the implementation sank under the weight of its own complexity, and the retailer claimed defeat, shuttering the project and swallowing the $500 million as a loss. (Read my blog post on this topic at *https://www.membrain.com/blog/how-to-make-the-mistakes-that-cost-a-german-grocer-500-million.*)

THE HYDRA IN THE SALES ORGANIZATION

The sales industry has been far from immune to the plague of the Hydra.

Let's return to the 1990s, with its increasing consolidation of CRM and ERP along with other sales and operations technologies, and the emergence of the one system to rule them all, the currently largest CRM company: Salesforce.

When Salesforce originally hit the market, it was the scrappy competitor to big, consolidated systems. This little cloud-based piece of software made it possible for small organizations to coordinate and collaborate more effectively and to share information more easily without heavy investments in on-site hardware and expensive engineers to manage it. They bashed large companies, like Oracle and Siebel, for being cumbersome and expensive monsters.

Today, Salesforce is the Hydra in our industry.

While it functions just fine as a CRM, a system of records, in order to make it effective as an enablement tool, Salesforce requires plug-ins and customizations. Each of these plug-ins and customizations introduces new layers of complexity.

Each layer costs money and time as new plug-ins and custom code are required to fix the problem or get the system to function as desired.

Meanwhile, instead of enabling salespeople with a streamlined tool that helps them sell, reduces willpower depletion, and provides coaching, the program forces them to navigate ever-increasing technological complexity, taking time away from actually selling, and reducing their willpower reserves with every work-around they have to navigate—much like the electronic health record has now done by taking doctors away from time with their patients.

The foundation of Salesforce is still operating on those bad assumptions:

- Salespeople are born, not made (so just give them data and let them do their thing).
- Salespeople are naturally self-disciplined (tell them to enter their data and use the system and they will).
- Sellers and buyers are logical creatures (so they'll do what makes sense even if they don't feel like it).

A thousand plug-ins and customizations are designed to combat these assumptions. Enablement functions and training plug-ins and reinforcement tools and on and on, but each time you plug in one of these so-called solutions to try to make the system treat your sales team like the humans they are, you create technological complexity that feeds the Hydra.

SALES TECHNOLOGY TODAY

Of course, CRM has come a long way since the 1990s. We have smartphones, marketing automation, and sophisticated automation.

Every day, new little sales applications, based on these emerging technologies and new ways of thinking about sales, enter the market. Each of them competes to get noticed by the market and, in turn, by the big technology companies. Most hope to get swallowed up into the Hydra so stakeholders can walk away with cash and leave the Hydra to grow the technology.

In order to do this, they have to sell enough licenses to be viewed as competitive. They market aggressively, and unwary companies buy them and add them to their stack. Call recording applications, org chart builders, email automation, scheduling apps, data enrichment software, sales content management, learning management systems, account planners, opportunity management tools, AI content delivery systems, and on and on.

Meanwhile, salespeople—the humans at the heart of the sales organization—continue to be human. They continue to lack self-discipline. They continue to be illogical. They continue to need guidance and coaching to be the best they can be.

They continue to be bogged down by a thousand technologies that try to take their jobs (automate everything!) and force them into submission while turning their day into a labyrinth of platforms, tools, and disconnected workflows that slow them down and prevent them from doing what they were hired to do.

THE EFFECTS OF THE HYDRA ON OUR SALES ORGANIZATIONS

If you've got a Hydra in your organization, you probably already know it. And it is hurting you even more than you realize. Here are some of the outcomes you may be seeing:

- CRM implementations that drag on forever
- Garbage data and unreliable sales forecasts
- Spotty or nonexistent implementation of sales processes
- Low user adoption of the CRM
- Poor retention of sales training
- Rogue salespeople doing what they think is best, ignoring best practices
- Making simple mistakes that kill deals
- Failing to record activities, making team collaboration difficult
- Using off-brand, or old, collateral with incorrect messaging
- Sales managers spending excessive time manipulating spreadsheets
- Difficulty pinpointing the root of sales effectiveness problems
- Flat performance—salespeople not getting substantially better over time
- Stressful work environment and high salesperson turnover

CRM today may seem indispensable to sales organizations, but it's also killing them in a thousand different ways. So what are we to do about it?

CAN THE HYDRA BE STOPPED?

The sales industry is not alone in suffering under the weight of bad assumptions and technological complexity. Healthcare, education, manufacturing—almost every industry, in fact—struggles against their respective Hydras, trying to create an environment where the technology serves the humans rather than the other way around.

Can the sales industry defeat its Hydra? Or, better yet, find a way to sail right past it and into clear waters where the fishing is good and the crew is happy?

The answer is yes. You can. And that's what the next chapters will show you.

6

STOP THE BLEEDING

So far, I have examined the ways in which human psychology and behavior undermine the success of a sales organization and how sales technology makes the problem worse.

Now, I'm going to flip the script and establish a framework that will harness human nature inside your sales organization, make technology the servant to the human, and achieve world-class sales performance as a result.

The first pillar of the framework comes out of the discipline of commercial aircraft flight via the discipline of medicine. As discussed in a previous chapter, medical errors are a leading cause of death in the United States. They kill more people in the country than auto accidents, stroke, diabetes, and pneumonia.

This happens despite the fact that medical professionals are among the most highly trained, committed, and technology-enabled professionals in the world and is one reason we know that discipline is a universally lacking quality among humans.

Atul Gawande, the American surgeon, writer, and public health researcher introduced in the previous chapter about technological complexity, is actually better known for a very simple, low-tech solution he pioneered to reduce hospital deaths: the checklist.

Gawande's journey to the checklist, which he details in his book *The Checklist Manifesto*, and its associated TED Talk "How Do We Heal Medicine," began with research into yet another industry with high risks and highly trained professionals: commercial airlines.

Air travel, like surgery, is a highly complex activity with many opportunities for tragic mistakes, from the design of the aircraft to construction, maintenance, air traffic control, and piloting.

Prior to the 1930s, flying was a dangerous activity reserved for only the brightest and bravest. Pilots were largely viewed as brave pioneers whose raw skill and knowledge combined with the power of their machines to keep their planes in flight.

But as aircraft became more complicated and commercial flights became common, passengers demanded assurances of safety. The commercial airline industry provided it.

Today, air travel is the world's safest mode of transit. Is this because everyone in the airline industry is more disciplined than anyone else? Of course not.

It's because they follow process, supported by checklists.

Every flight follows a very specific set of processes, from how the aircraft system is checked and maintained, to the steps pilots take before, during, and after the flight. These processes are divided into workflows, and each one is accompanied by a checklist. Everyone on the flight team has the power to stop the process at any point if something on the checklist isn't complete or there is a red flag issue.

FIG 1.11 Simple checklists make commercial aircraft one of the safest modes of travel available.

Gawande had the insight that the same two tools could have a similar effect on the practice of medicine and especially surgery. He created standard workflows and checklists for his surgical teams, based on every process from pre-op to post-op. He empowered nurses and technicians to hold surgeons accountable to their checklists.

It worked.

In the surgical units where checklists were implemented, preventable death rates plummeted by 47 percent. The technique spread to other medical teams and other hospitals, with similarly outstanding results.

For instance, in 2004, the state of Michigan found that infection rates for patients in their ICUs exceeded national averages. In an effort to improve their record, they implemented checklists in all of their intensive care units for just one process: inserting IV lines. Within three months, the infection rate in Michigan hospitals' ICUs decreased by 66 percent. In fact, it fell so low that the average Michigan unit outperformed 90 percent of ICUs nationwide, saving an estimated $175 million and more than 1,500 lives.

THE SIMPLE SECRET TO STOP THE BLEEDING IN YOUR SALES ORGANIZATION

As we have seen, salespeople, like surgeons, pilots, and other humans, are not naturally self-disciplined, and they aren't born knowing what to do.

Establishing a formal process, with checklists and reinforcement, is the key to harnessing their human strengths while managing their human weaknesses. It's especially critical now as sales complexity continues to increase and b2b sales require teams to work together to bring in business.

When your sales teams have a well-organized and effective structure with checklists and reinforcement for routine behaviors, you free up their intelligence to focus on the unique circumstances of each sale.

Of course, in order to be effective, the processes and checklists have to align with the work that actually needs to be done. Next, let's review the essential steps to establishing effective processes and checklists inside your organization.

ALIGN STRATEGY, PROCESS, AND METHODOLOGY

To be effective, your sales team's guiding structure must be built on a foundation of effective sales strategy. Then process and methodologies can be built to align with and support that strategy.

 There are many books available to help you develop an effective sales strategy, and I've recommended a few in the Read More section at the end of this book. I also encourage you to download my white paper comparing and contrasting the top methodologies from ***https://stop.killing.deals/resources.***

Because so much has already been written about these topics, I will confine my discussion here to one key point: The sales process is not just a drop-down menu in your CRM.

Many organizations think they have a sales process because they have a list of stages into which to categorize opportunities, with category names such as "prospect," "qualified," "presentation," "proposal," and "won/lost."

Such a method of categorizing may be somewhat useful for analyzing the pipeline (though most sales leaders will agree that the key word here is somewhat), it's not a true process unless each stage is associated with clearly defined entry and exit criteria, milestones, steps, and activities.

In order to establish a milestone-based process that is capable of guiding your salespeople through your way of selling, download the Sales Process Builder from **https://stop.killing.deals/resources.**

ORGANIZE YOUR SALES PROCESS(ES) INTO LOGICAL WORKFLOWS

When a medical professional walks into the pre-op area to prepare for surgery, there are certain specific steps they are supposed to take to ensure the safety of the patient long before the operation actually begins. These steps must be taken in a specific order and comply with specific criteria. For instance: wash hands for a certain amount of time in a certain temperature of water with a certain type of soap, after dressing for surgery but before entering the operating room.

The how and when of each activity is critical, and more or less the same every time. Once surgery has begun, a similar stepwise process continues to be active, but changing conditions may require the medical team to make adjustments to their activities and approach as they go.

It is critical to the operating team's effectiveness that they all follow the same process, that they hand off activities in a logical fashion, and that they understand at all times which part of the process they are engaged in and whether the process is dynamic or static at that stage.

Likewise, in an optimal environment, a sales team will always know where in the process a project is, be aligned with decision-makers, know how and when to hand off activities, and what specific activities each should be involved in as well as where they should use their skills and intelligence to adapt to changing conditions.

To ensure a smooth handling of each part of the process, it's important first to identify and separate the different workflows that each member of your team engages in. Just as pre-operative procedures dictate a different workflow from procedures during the operation, so also sales workflows can be logically divided into segments.

In most b2b sales organizations, the sales team engages in at least three primary workflows, each with their own activities and contexts, plus a final process, to analyze and optimize:

1. Prospecting and qualifying (Earn the right)

2. Opportunity management (Achieve consensus)

3. Account planning (Proactive growth)

4. Analyzing and optimizing (Continuously)

Each of these workflows has its own rhythm and needs and should be handled as separate workflows. In some cases, each workflow may be handled by different people in the organization, while in others each salesperson may handle all aspects.

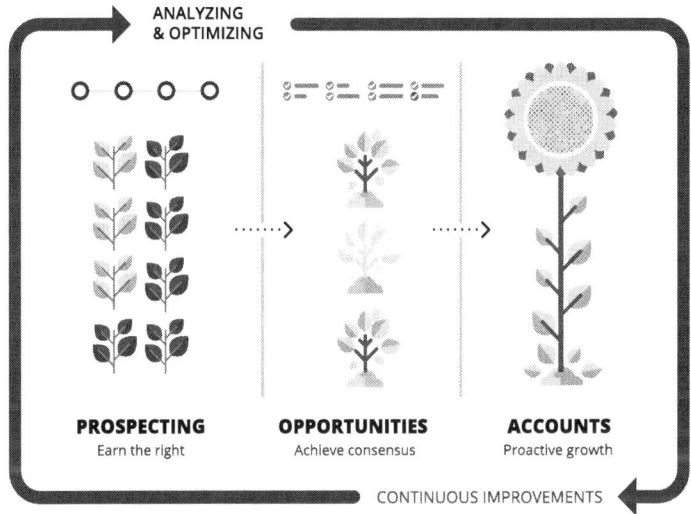

FIG 1.12 Each sales workflow has its own rhythm and needs.

THE PROSPECTING WORKFLOW

Activities in the prospecting stage may include online research, cold calls, email, LinkedIn engagement, meetings, and any other activities designed to gain access to and evaluate potential clients.

In this workflow, activity levels are usually high, and efficiency is important. It's critical that this workflow makes it easy for salespeople to engage in the right activities at the right volume to find and qualify or disqualify prospects quickly and effectively, according to the right criteria. Prospecting can be done for inbound leads or outbound for both new and existing clients.

Failures at this stage of the process can result either in too few prospects, or pipelines bloated with unqualified candidates.

A properly designed workflow for prospecting will help salespeople to quickly find and engage potential prospects and accurately qualify them as early as possible. It should reinforce standard criteria for qualification, and prospects should only be allowed to move into the second workflow once they have fully met those criteria.

This helps salespeople to operate effectively and efficiently and also leads to good clean pipeline data from which to forecast and report.

THE OPPORTUNITY AND PIPELINE MANAGEMENT WORKFLOW

Only fully qualified prospects should ever be moved into this workflow, as this is where we start forecasting revenues. Once a salesperson does move a prospect into the opportunity workflow, it should guide them through every milestone so that they are never left wondering or trying to remember, "Okay, what do I do next?"

It is especially important that this workflow is based around progress, not just activity. Just because a salesperson has made eighty calls to a client does not mean that they've made progress. It should guide salespeople clearly through all of the critical steps, milestones, and stages of your sales process (which in turn needs to ensure alignment with how the buyer will make their decision) and reinforce adherence to them.

As not all steps and milestones can be predicted, the workflow also needs to be dynamic to change based on the selling situation and be autonomous to allow the salesperson to add to it when necessary.

THE ACCOUNT PLANNING WORKFLOW

Once you have won an account, or in order to win it in the first place, you need to invest time researching and understanding their business and how to be of maximum value to the client. This workflow includes understanding their company structure, their key initiatives, specifics about their industry and competitors, who's who, what you've helped them with in the past, and what you could do to increase your engagement. This workflow revolves around discovering and organizing information and creating logical connections among disparate sources of information, some of which may be entered by multiple members of the sales team.

The data accumulated in this workflow as well as the ability to add to it, need to be available to anyone on the team at any point in the process. That's why it is critical that this workflow operates independently of the others.

ANALYZING AND OPTIMIZING

If your team is to continually improve performance, analysis and optimization must become part of your routine procedures. This workflow should focus on tools and steps that enable analysis of data from the project, and a consistent approach to asking questions that help uncover the reasons for wins and losses.

This workflow should be separate from the others, but the data and insights from it should feed back into the rest of the process in order to improve strategy, skills, processes, and coaching.

INTEGRATE WITH YOUR UNIQUE WAY OF SELLING

Some organizations may have additional processes and workflows, depending on the type of sales motion necessary. For instance, you may approach new customers differently from existing ones, or one business unit may sell solutions at a higher complexity than another.

These factors, along with your workflows and processes, can become your unique way of selling, a differentiating factor against your competition.

Dividing your processes into logical workflows according to your unique way of selling will help everyone on your team to this:

- Better organize their time and activities
- More quickly access the information and enablement they need
- See where help, coaching, and resources are needed
- Create and utilize better quality data

INTRODUCE A SHARED SALES LANGUAGE

If you ask two salespeople on your team the difference between a lead and a prospect, will you get the same answer twice? What about the definition of qualified? Do they know your ideal customer fit? Would they describe your sales process the same way? If not, then your sales team does not have a shared language.

Shared language is critical to team functioning as well as to effective data collection and analysis. The specific words you use to discuss aspects of your sales process matter, but what matters more is that you agree on the definition of those words.

The same is true for methodologies. There are many wonderful methodologies available, but any of them can be beneficial to your team as long as you're all using the same words to describe what you are doing.

A shared language makes it possible to accurately understand the forecasted pipeline and to compare key performance indicators such as win rate, deal size, and sales cycle length. What to call key stakeholders and how to understand and capture their attitude and influence and their sense of urgency is also critically important.

ASSOCIATE CHECKLISTS WITH EACH STAGE, STEP, AND MILESTONE OF THE PROCESS AND EMBED THEM INTO THE WORKFLOWS

One of the biggest causes of medically induced injuries and deaths is skipped steps. A technician doesn't drape the patient properly. A doctor doesn't double-check an incision site against a fail-safe. A nurse doesn't confirm a medication with the patient's chart and wristband before administering a medication.

The same mistakes happen in sales, and the solution is equally simple. Once your process is embedded into the salesperson's workflow, you can associate checklists with each step and re-quire salespeople to complete checklists before moving to the next step. These checklist steps can, and should, also include information on how to best perform them. These small things alone will make a massive difference. I promise.

Empower everyone on the sales team to call a halt to the sales process if a checklist item has not been completed or reveals information that justifies disqualifying or walking away from a sales project. This simple step eliminates mistakes like jump-ing too soon to a presentation, failing to engage all the right stakeholders, and spending too little time on discovery.

Once you've established a straightforward process and asso-ciated checklists to its critical workflows, it's time to move to the next step in healing your sales organization, with a holistic approach to sales enablement.

7 HEAL THE ORGANIZATION WITH ENABLEMENT

Once you have stopped the bleeding in your organization, you can move to the next stage, which is to establish a holistic sales enablement system that builds your sales team into a healthy, thriving, and continuously improving organization.

Before I get into the details of how to do that, it's important that we speak the same language. Currently, the term sales enablement is often used to talk about serving up content to salespeople during the sales process. I want to encourage you to think about the term much more holistically.

WHAT IS SALES ENABLEMENT?

Ask twenty sales experts the question, and you'll get
twenty answers. I know, because I did it and com-
piled the results in a white paper called "What Shall
Sales Enablement Enable?" Feel free to download it
from ***https://stop.killing.deals/resources.***

When viewed holistically, as we must if we want to develop truly world-class sales organizations, sales enablement
means giving your team the support it needs to make more
sales, faster, and more profitable.

Simple to say, difficult to execute.

In a complex b2b environment, sales enablement means
making sure that everyone on the team has exactly what
they need and when they need it in order to do the best job
they can possibly do to achieve their goals. Beyond sales and
marketing content, which is important, this also includes
training, messaging, process guidance, coaching, analytics,
and technologies and tools.

More than the sum of its parts, effective sales enablement execution is the orchestration of all those efforts and more, into
a simple, unified system that is easy for salespeople, and their
managers, to navigate. Holistic and effective sales enablement helps salespeople and sales organizations achieve their
goals, without weighing them down.

A tall order but achievable with the right framework. Having
developed your process for each workflow and associated

checklists with each, you're already part of the way there. Think of those elements as the foundation of a sales enablement structure. With construction as our analogy, the next step then is to frame the structure.

Here's a five-step plan on how to do that.

1. USE YOUR PROCESS AND CHECKLISTS TO ASSESS YOUR SALES TEAM AND ENVIRONMENT

Start with your customer-focused sales process and associated checklists, as designed, using the steps in the last chapter. For every step and item on each checklist, ask yourself whether your organization and your sales team has everything they need to fully and expertly execute as designed.

Some common questions you'll want to ask during this stage include these:

- What is preventing our sales team from excelling at each step and stage?

- Would buyers pay for the advice and assistance given by our team? Are they having valuable interactions with my team?

- Does everyone have access to the tools and information they need to complete each element of this process and checklist?

- Is everyone on the team sitting in the right seats, with the right capabilities and mindsets to execute on the parts of the process they are responsible for?

This assessment will quickly reveal for you where your greatest areas of weakness are. You'll especially want to examine these areas, which represent some of the most common gaps on sales teams:

- Poor recruitment and onboarding processes
- Wrong people
- Wrong seats
- Missing skills
- Bad habits
- Unsupportive beliefs

POOR RECRUITMENT AND ONBOARDING

In the first chapter of this book, I described some of the costly mistakes I have made in building sales teams. The underlying reasons for those mistakes were the same faulty assumptions that most sales organizations and leaders make.

Because I believed salespeople are born, not made, I underestimated the difference between a simple and a complex sales environment and how our shift to the latter requires different approaches and different traits in salespeople. Hence, when recruiting, I was looking for the wrong traits. I also failed, for the same reason, to provide an effective onboarding program.

Because I overestimated my team's skills and self-discipline and underestimated the role of emotions in their behavior and our buyers' decision-making, I did not equip my sales team with a well-designed and reinforced sales process, nor did I do a good job with coaching.

Needless to say, I was making things very hard for myself and my new recruits.

To reduce recruitment mistakes, use a sales-specific assessment, like those available through the Objective Management Group (objectivemanagement.com), to ensure you're hiring for the right traits for your environment. These and similar assessments can also help you with the next two areas of potential weakness by determining whether you have the right people in the right seats now.

WRONG PEOPLE

Individuals on your sales team should be a good fit for the complexity of your sales environment, your culture and values as well as with the other individuals on your team. This means that just because someone was a superstar on another sales team, doesn't mean they belong on yours.

Unfortunately, quite often, even a superstar salesperson can be a wrong match for your team. When that happens, their presence in your organization can be like a cancerous growth that infects the whole team.

Signs of a wrong-person problem are:

- Excessive conflict
- Bad attitudes
- Resentment
- Lack of cooperation
- Cowboy behaviors—someone who insists on doing it their own way even when they've been trained differently, and who resists coaching

One way to identify the wrong-person people on your team is to compare each of your team members against your values and other measures you identify as important to their success. In a complex b2b environment, for instance, the right salespeople are usually collaborative, growth-oriented, process-oriented, and coachable. They have healthy attitudes about themselves, their roles, and their willingness to change and learn.

Identifying the wrong people on your team can be painful, but letting them go can free up a lot of energy and time on your team and ultimately is critical to moving forward into healthier functioning.

WRONG SEATS

Sometimes an employee may be a good fit for your organization, but a bad fit for the position they're in. Some examples include

- An account manager better suited in a customer support role
- A person focused on new business who should be nurturing existing accounts
- A sales manager who really just wants to win big deals and be the hero

To assess whether you have the right people in the wrong seats, identify your top performers in each role, or use external benchmarks, then develop a list of characteristics and skills they share that make them good at that role. Measure everyone in that role against your list and either move, upskill, or let go of anyone who doesn't fit.

MISSING SKILLS

Many sales organizations spend enormous amounts of money on training and skills building for their teams. Most of that money is wasted, and one of the key reasons is that the training isn't aligned with what salespeople actually need in order to perform better, nor well reinforced in daily operations.

Because you now have a clearly articulated sales process, you can measure sales skills against those necessary to effectively execute, and now you can identify where your gaps are. Use this process to uncover what skills are needed, who needs them, and how urgent the need is.

BAD HABITS

Are your salespeople jumping to presentation too quickly? Are they failing to uncover and help buyers make decisions? Are they not uncovering and communicating with all the stakeholders? Are they using old, off-brand messaging or focusing all their time on existing customers without spending enough time with potential new prospects? Are they only using email and social media to connect instead of picking up the phone?

Use your process and checklists to measure what salespeople are actually doing in the field against what they ought to be doing and to identify any bad habits that need to be adjusted. Most salespeople do develop bad habits along the way, and measuring and identifying them this way will enable you to address them systematically.

UNSUPPORTIVE BELIEFS

Your beliefs about yourself and about your role impact your ability to perform. A person who believes that they are capable, competent, and deserving of success is more likely to behave in capable and competent ways and to earn the success they believe they deserve.

A landmark study about the Health Belief Model showed that people who held a view of themselves as capable and effective (high in self-efficacy) were more successful in achieving positive health goals for themselves than those who scored low on self-efficacy.

In the sales context, this suggests that people on your team who "believe in themselves" really are more likely to perform better. A salesperson who believes they deserve to make big sales will more likely make big sales. A coach who believes they deserve their sales team's trust will more likely win their team's trust.

Symptoms of unsupportive beliefs manifest in these ways:

- Salespeople who engage in all the right activities but don't get results (may not believe in their right to success)

- Sales team members who resist change even when it's clear that it will be positive change (may not believe in their own power to get better)

- Salespeople who say they want to get better but don't take actions to do so (may not believe in their ability to improve)

- Salespeople who regularly ask for steep discounts (may not believe in the value of your offerings or are uncomfortable talking about money)

Once you have identified these and any other gaps in your organization's ability to execute on your process and checklists, you can move on to prioritizing and developing a plan to address them.

2. PRIORITIZE YOUR NEEDS AND DEVELOP A TREATMENT PLAN

Some patients only need a little supportive care to reach the next level of health after an injury. Others need a lot. In many cases, treatments must be organized and prioritized to ensure the patient enjoys the full benefit.

Likewise, your sales environment assessment will likely reveal some areas where there is an immediate and critical need, and other areas that just need a little support eventually, and many areas in between.

Based on your gaps and priorities, develop a treatment plan that will close your most critical gaps immediately and work toward closing the rest in a logical fashion. Your treatment plan will likely include these steps:

- Recruitment and onboarding improvement
- Skills development
- Workflow support
- Coaching
- Moving team members to better seats

Remember to measure your priorities against the needs of your process to ensure that your sales team members are constantly improving toward better execution of your strategy.

3. REINFORCE NEW PROCESSES AND SKILLS WITH EMBEDDED TRAINING IN CONTEXT

Too much sales training occurs in a vacuum. Salespeople go offsite for a day or two, get loaded up with training content, and then come back to the office and are expected to implement what they learned in their daily life.

Some salespeople may manage to remember the training for a while, but rubber banding is more common than not.

 The spacing effect discussed in our cognitive biases white paper is relevant here: *https://stop.killing.deals/resources.*

People are more likely to remember information that is spread out and repeated over time, in small chunks, than information that is dumped all at once in a sales training session in a crowded, hot hotel training room with bad coffee.

The forgetting curve, published by Hermann Ebbinghaus in 1885 (that is not a typo) makes this reality visual. When you memorize information, your recall of that information will be high immediately after committing it to memory and then drops quickly. Unless the information is reinforced over time, you will barely remember more than 20 percent after one month.

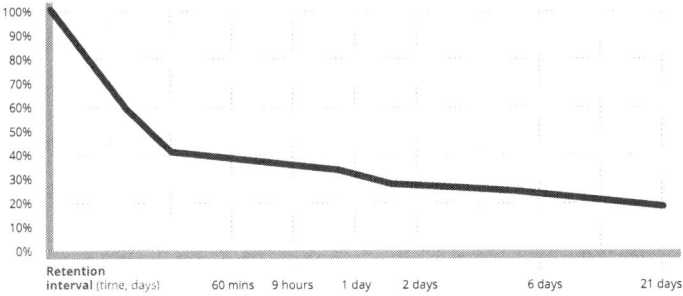

Percentage retained

FIG 1.13 Ebbinghaus's forgetting curve.

When reinforcement occurs at regular intervals, recall increases. After each reminder, we retain more of the information, considering that it is relevant and understandable to us.

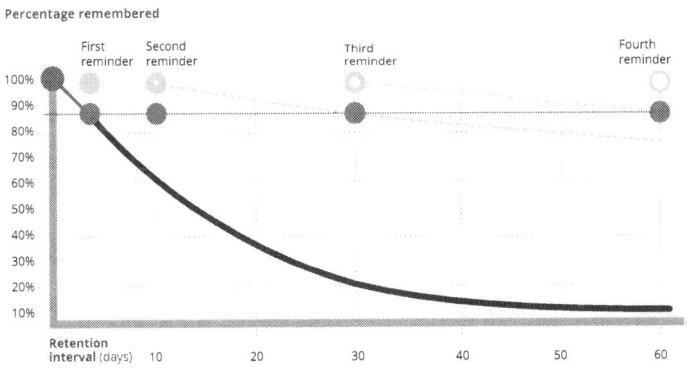

Percentage remembered

FIG 1.14 The Learning Curve: reinforcement helps us remember.

Your process and checklists established in the previous chapter provide the foundation on which you can build reinforcement. The workflow processes and checklists can guide your sales team through the essential elements of their training and skills. Then you can build bite-sized chunks of reinforcement training into the process to remind them directly when each piece of training is relevant to their workflow.

By bringing their training directly into the process at the time when they need it, you substantially improve their recall and their commitment to applying the new skills and abilities.

4. INTELLIGENTLY INTEGRATE CONTEXT-BASED SALES COLLATERAL INTO THE WORKFLOWS

Here is where most organizations start and stop with sales enablement. They think of it as simply delivering up sales content when the salespeople need it. While this is not the only aspect of sales enablement that matters, it does matter.

Why? Because most sales and marketing organizations create a lot more enablement content than salespeople ever actually use. They may have presentations, case studies, white papers, ebooks, newsletters, demo videos, and much more that they have invested in but that most of their salespeople never actually use.

Or the collateral is the wrong collateral or there's not enough of it or it's not useful for what salespeople are actually doing in the field.

Some sales organizations have attempted to solve this problem with automated sales enablement systems. Unfortunately, these often fail to deliver on their promises. Without a solid and dynamic process in place, the AI has nothing to learn from and could be worse than no enablement at all.

In other cases, sales organizations have taken a page from the marketing book and inundate buyers with sales enablement material automatically through these "intelligent" systems. This is the worst case possible, as it causes buyer fatigue, undermines trust, and can interfere with the seller's hard-won relationship.

For these reasons, it's best to leave automated messages to the marketing department and use content enablement to augment what your salespeople are doing and to help them make good decisions, rather than to take over this important function.

To do this, use your sales process again to map the sales collateral that is most useful at each step and stage. Then tag content and make it easy for salespeople to access and use it at the moment when they need it.

With a well-designed set of processes and workflows, this sequencing becomes an easier task, as you can use context clues for each situation based on where it is in the process, the competitors, industry, pain points, and other factors to make intelligent suggestions to salespeople, and then let them use their good judgment to share what matters with the customer.

Make it possible for them to do this without leaving their workflow, to avoid slowing them down, and you will have a sales content delivery system that actually enables your team to perform better.

While every organization is different, the essential steps in the process of building your content delivery system are as follows:

1. Organize your existing marketing content assets.

2. Analyze what's missing and outdated against your sales process.

3. Create missing assets and update outdated ones.

4. Tag each content piece with the right contexts in sales team workflows (industry, persona, competitor, etc.).

5. Have your sales technology serve content suggestions to each salesperson based on these contexts.

6. Make it easy to search and find the right content at all times.

7. Make it easy for them to use the content from directly inside their workflow.

8. Track what they use, its success, and analyze these data constantly to improve content and content suggestions.

5. MAKE WORKFLOWS BEAUTIFUL AND INTUITIVE

Beauty and enjoyment may seem like fluffy topics, with no place in a book about sales performance. But these two aspects, beauty and enjoyment, actually serve an extremely practical purpose, which you can harness to supercharge your team's performance.

Have you ever sat by the beach reading a great book and been surprised to find that the sun was setting and it was time to go home? Been skiing and, while going downhill and enjoying the scenery, you realized an entire day had passed in what seemed like minutes?

Do you have a favorite hobby you can lose yourself in for hours?

When we're in the flow of an activity, everything seems easy and straightforward. Flow also has the effect of reducing or eliminating willpower fatigue. You never have to exert willpower to keep doing something you're in the flow of doing.

Flow also improves performance and increases stamina.

The delicious altered state of consciousness called flow can be difficult to achieve and even harder to maintain, but a truly world-class enablement system can help.

8 STRENGTHEN THE TEAM WITH EFFECTIVE COACHING

Having completed the steps to this point, your next step is to integrate your system into a beautiful, easy-to-use, intuitive workflow that your salespeople love to use. Remove obstacles that force them to switch between applications or otherwise task-switch frequently, and put each next step right in front of them when they need it, like a nurse handing a scalpel to a surgeon.

Such a system removes a great deal of the friction that inhibits flow and sets your salespeople up to gain momentum and focus and to enjoy the adrenaline high inherent in doing a challenging job well and efficiently.

In fact, all of the elements of this chapter and the previous one work together to induce and enhance your salespeople's state of flow toward higher and higher performance. By taking these steps, you free up their brainpower to make better and better decisions and to create stronger relationships with your customers. You've given them the skills they need to perform—and the structure within which to apply them.

But to achieve truly world-class performance, you need one more element: world-class coaching.

Many organizations treat coaching as an afterthought or an intervention when a salesperson is struggling. In other cases, coaching is approached as though it were merely a warm, fuzzy nice-to-have bonus to offer when it's convenient.

In still other organizations, coaching isn't offered at all.

This is a mistake.

Just like a winning sports team won't ever become a world-class competitor without a top-notch coach, so too your organization cannot become a world-class performer without a winning coaching system.

Most organizations, even if they believe in sound coaching, don't have the structure in place to deliver it effectively. But your organization is different. Unlike your competitors, your coaching can be built upon a firm foundation of process and checklists and executed within the structure of effective sales enablement as outlined in this book.

Implement the steps to this point, and you will have a framework in place to make your coaching system the multiplier that delivers exponential results against investment.

At this level, coaching becomes the lynchpin that:

- Addresses the human factors on your team
- Clears obstacles
- Reinforces sales process and methodology
- Supports skill growth
- Improves ramp-up times
- Reduces turnover
- Reinforces positive sales culture
- Increases retention of high performers
- Creates feedback loops for continual improvement
- And yields major competitive advantage

Using the framework outlined in the previous chapters, here's how to take your team to the next level with an effective coaching system, starting with the misunderstandings about coaching that you must avoid along the way.

WHAT SALES COACHING IS NOT

There are a lot of misunderstandings about what sales coaching is and is not, so let's get the big ones out of the way right now. Sales coaching is not management, it is not training, it is not performing, and it is not mentoring.

Here's what those four tasks look like, and why they're not the same as coaching.

- Management: Management is filing reports, conducting performance reviews, hiring and firing, and putting employees on notice. These are all activities of a sales manager, but they are not coaching.

- Teaching and telling: Teaching and telling involve standing in front of a group to give them all the same information. This can be an important aspect of sales training, but it is not coaching.

- Performing: Sales managers, who were often high-performing salespeople before they were managers, often find it tempting to step in and "just do it for them" when a salesperson is struggling. They may justify it as leading by example, but this is performing, not coaching, and in fact can be detrimental to the relationship and the salesperson's growth.

- Mentoring: A mentor can be a valuable asset for any professional, but there is a difference between mentoring and coaching. A mentor generally focuses on the whole person and their large dreams and achievements in life, often based on the mentor's own experiences. A coach can be a mentor also, but a coach's primary responsibility is to the salesperson's immediate responsibilities and goals. A coach is also responsible for the whole team, and not just a few mentees. And, although the coach's work can overlap with the mentor's when it comes to looking at life goals, the coach's primary focus remains on the steps and skills and behaviors necessary for the salesperson to make performance improvements.

Management, training, performing, and mentoring are all important functions in a successful sales organization, but it is important to understand coaching as a critical function separate and apart from these other functions.

WHAT SALES COACHING IS

Sales coaching, in its best and most effective manifestation, is an activity often conducted by a sales manager who is focused on helping the entire team achieve their highest potential as a sales team.

FIG 1.15 Sales coaching is focused on helping individuals achieve their highest potential.

To be effective coaching must be:

- Individual: Coaching focuses on identifying strengths, weaknesses, and constraints for individual salespeople and providing them with customized questions to steer them toward their goals.

- Supportive: Coaching focuses on selling through, not for. It helps salespeople find the right resources and gain the right skills to overcome their own challenges.

- Proactive: Effective sales coaches don't wait for their salespeople to have problems before providing coaching.

- Prioritized: An effective coaching system prioritizes coaching time, ensuring that managers are freed to engage in this important activity.

- Team-focused: An effective coach has to believe in their people, care about the success of others and the team as a whole, and want to guide others toward their own solutions and personal growth. It is a mindset as well as an activity.

The best coaches don't get into the game and play, they provide the resources, guidance, accountability, and help bring out the motivation for their team members to perform at their best. Then they stand on the sidelines and cheer (and sometimes shout).

It's time to establish the structure that will make your coaching system the best in your class.

HOW TO BUILD AN EFFECTIVE COACHING STRUCTURE

An effective coaching structure starts with the process, checklists, and enablement structure developed in the last two chapters. With those elements established, your coaching system can become systematized, based on quality data and feedback from your enablement system that is consistent, and highly effective. Here's how to build it.

FOCUS ON MINDSET

Start by promoting people with the right mindset and continue by reinforcing that mindset on the management team. This means that your organization must give up the knee-jerk practice of promoting high performers into management and focus on finding the people who already demonstrate the right mentality for coaching.

A person with the right coaching mentality will:

- Consistently and cheerfully collaborate with others
- Share information rather than hoarding it
- Engage informally in coaching and helping other salespeople
- Genuinely care about all of the other people in the organization
- Be willing and eager to learn new skill sets
- Consistently demonstrate a greater interest in the success of their team than in getting credit for their own contributions
- Be comfortable with technologies for analyzing and interpreting information to enable coaching

Many organizations find this shift uncomfortable, especially if salespeople already feel that a management promotion is the natural next step for a high performer. Take the time to restructure the way your team thinks about promotion. Look for ways to reward high performers in a more productive manner, while reserving management promotions for people with the right mindset.

With the right people in management, reinforce the coaching mindset with training and support. Reward coaches when their teams improve and when they actively engage in productive coaching behaviors. Don't reward cowboy or other behaviors that undermine the coaching mindset.

If you already have managers with the wrong mindset, and you think they have the potential to be better managers, help them transition from the need to be heroes in the sales force to helping other people become the heroes.

MAKE COACHING A PRIORITY

One of the biggest obstacles to effective coaching is the belief that it doesn't really matter. Even organizations that give lip service to the importance of coaching often don't invest in it at the level they invest in other aspects of the organization.

In order to build an effective system, you must first believe that coaching is important and decide to invest in it. It won't happen overnight, and it won't happen without a commitment.

Once sales leadership has identified coaching as a priority, then that mindset must be propagated throughout the organization. Teach managers that coaching is one of their highest priorities and free them of excessive reporting and other duties that get in the way of time for coaching. Encourage them to plan and prepare their coaching efforts to make the most impact.

Teach them that coaching is not a separate activity that must be placed in a corner and attended to as a side duty, but that coaching is central to their role in the organization. Provide them with resources and encouragement to engage in coaching as part of their daily dealings with salespeople. Gradually, coaching should become a part of every interaction with salespeople, from a casual meeting on an elevator to a weekly sales pipeline review and win/loss meetings.

EXECUTE ACROSS MULTIPLE PRACTICE AREAS AND LEVELS

One of the reasons the sales profession is often viewed as more of an art than a science is that selling is incredibly complex. There are so many skills involved across so many areas that when a salesperson gets it absolutely right, the art of sales can look like magic.

An effective coaching program addresses all of these areas to provide salespeople with support and growth across all of them. Salespeople must have solid business acumen and be skilled in account planning, call planning, prospecting, reporting, qualifying, buying facilitation, consensus building, competitive analysis, and much more. Within each area are a huge number of variables and related skills that they must master.

For instance, the following six segments demonstrate how you can begin to address multiple areas and levels of coaching:

1. STRATEGY

At the strategic level, the coach focuses on the salesperson's goals and aspirations. These conversations help the salesperson to align their own motivations with the goals set by the organization. They should be both motivational and aspirational, encouraging the salesperson at a deep level to want to succeed and to believe that they can succeed.

2. PLANNING

In the planning area, coaches help salespeople understand the process they must follow to implement their strategic vision as well as what to do during specific portions of the sales process. Coaching in this area includes pre-call planning as well as post-call debriefing, and general planning to improve pipeline and progress through the sales process.

3. SKILLS AND ATTITUDE

This coaching level requires the coach to pay close attention to each salesperson's gaps and weaknesses in skills and attitudes. This can be done through analytics, listening in on calls, ride-alongs, and probing questions. Coaches should also be trained in recognizing limiting beliefs that may prevent salespeople from reaching the goals they set for themselves. At this level, coaches can point salespeople at resources for developing the skills and attitudes they need and help them access those resources. Then they must hold them accountable to their commitments.

4. PIPELINE

At this level, coaches have their eyes on the size, quality, and velocity of each salesperson's pipeline. They should be watching both leading and lagging indicators so that they can step in as soon as possible when there's a problem or weakness. When pipeline health lags, a good coach is proactive in approaching the salesperson and helping them to identify for themselves where the problem is and how to address it. Then the coach should be equipped and trained to follow up actively to ensure that the agreed-upon remedy is acted on by the salesperson.

5. ACCOUNTS AND OPPORTUNITIES

At this level, coaches may respond reactively to problems that salespeople bring to them, but should also work proactively in regular opportunity review meetings. During these meetings, smart coaches guide the salesperson to identify potential barriers, slowdowns, and other gaps in each account or opportunity and to develop approaches and next steps for each.

6. ACTIVITY

Alert coaches keep their fingers on the pulse of each salesperson's activities. They use the information from conversations to help salespeople see which activities they should engage in as well as how many and how often. This coaching helps salespeople improve their velocity. This level also includes helping salespeople perform activities in the most productive way, with call planning, call coaching, and other activity-oriented coaching.

A sales coach's job is not one for the fainthearted. Effective coaching is complex and layered, and the most successful coaches are well trained and supported in executing in all areas.

ADDRESS THE LOGICAL LEVELS OF CHANGE

Some athletes have everything it takes physically to reach the highest levels of the game, but they never do. In the sports world, this is a recognized phenomenon often talked about as mindset. In other cases, an athlete with less physical aptitude can sometimes outmatch competitors due to a strong mindset.

The same thing is true in any other endeavor, including sales.

To truly free your sales team to perform at world-class levels, you have to understand them as human beings. Your coaching program must treat each sales team member as a holistic being, helping them to address limiting beliefs, cognitive biases, and all the other human factors that impact performance.

Additionally, the coaching team must understand and work at the right level of change. Neuro-Linguistic Programming (NLP) describes the fundamental dynamics between mind (neuro) and language (linguistic) and how their interplay affects our body and behavior (programming). NLP introduces a number of models, including the logical levels of change model, which demonstrates how people change at different levels.

At the bottom levels, you may be able to make changes fairly easily, such as to environment or behavior. But these changes are rarely lasting if they are contrary to something at a higher level, such as a belief or identity, and these bottom-level changes rarely cause changes higher up the pyramid.

On the other hand, at the top levels of identity, beliefs, and values, change is hard, but once those changes are made, they tend to last, and they tend to impact all the lower levels as well.

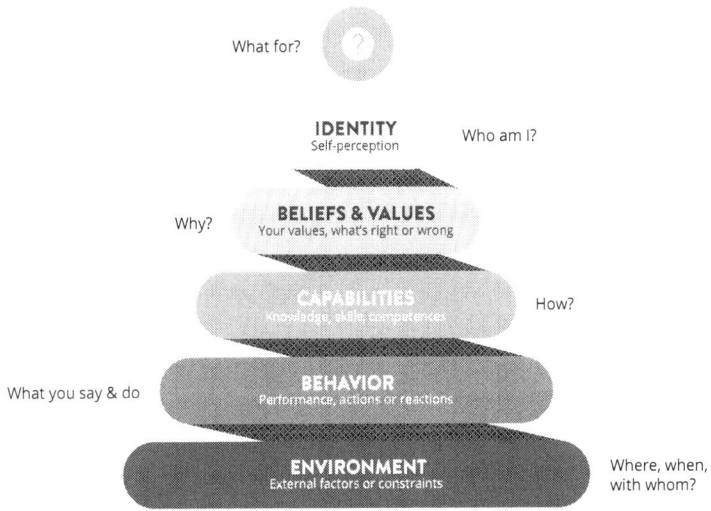

What for?

IDENTITY
Self-perception

Who am I?

Why?

BELIEFS & VALUES
Your values, what's right or wrong

CAPABILITIES
Knowledge, skills, competences

How?

What you say & do

BEHAVIOR
Performance, actions or reactions

ENVIRONMENT
External factors or constraints

Where, when, with whom?

FIG 1.16 t

It's a common mistake, when a salesperson is faltering, to try to change their behavior at a lower level without addressing more important aspects of their conscious and subconscious minds at the higher levels.

For instance, we may change their environment, expecting that a new headset or a new office space will give them a nudge in the right direction. Or we may insist on new behaviors, only to discover they quickly bounce back to old behaviors.

If we're not addressing the beliefs, values, identity, and purpose that drive them, any changes we make in their behaviors or environment will be short-lived with limited effectiveness.

For example, a salesperson who has limiting beliefs around their identity as a salesperson will never perform to the height of their capabilities. And a salesperson who believes their life purpose is not to be a salesperson will definitely never achieve the highest levels of performance.

A truly inspiring coaching program looks at each salesperson as a human being and helps them understand their own mindsets, limiting beliefs, biases, and other factors, and then gives them tools to shift into more powerful mindsets, more supportive beliefs, and thus into behaviors that counteract their biases and unsupportive human tendencies.

TRAIN COACHES TO ASK THE RIGHT QUESTIONS

Instead of focusing on telling salespeople what to do, an effective coach focuses on helping them discover for themselves the right actions to take.

To do this, coaches must be trained to ask revealing questions in every area and at every level. Questioning should dig deep and not settle for surface answers. Probing questions help salespeople articulate for themselves what's holding them back and encourage them at a conscious and subconscious level to take ownership of the solution.

The following table shows possible questions in each of six areas. These should not be viewed as an exhaustive list but merely as an illustration of the depth and variety of questions coaches can employ. Note also that even within these sample areas, there is overlap and that some questions from one area can be equally valuable in another.

COACHING QUESTIONS BY PRACTICE AREA

Strategy	Skills & Attitude	Pipeline	Opportunity & Account	Call Planning
What will success look like for you and the company?	Would your customers pay to access your knowledge? Why or why not?	How is your pipeline doing? Are you happy with its size and health? How would you like it to be different?	Why should the potential customer even care about this?	What is your next action to get progress toward...?
What is the main outcome you would like to achieve?	What value do you bring to a prospect's business? Is it valuable enough?	Why does your pipeline include these specific deals?	What would cause a potential customer to do nothing? How strong is the incumbent?	What have you tried so far? What else could you try?
How will you know you've reached that outcome?	What skill or knowledge do you need to achieve...?	Are there any opportunities in your pipeline that aren't as promising as you originally thought?	How can you reach the people you want to talk to?	What is the likelihood of X happening?
Will these outcomes make you a better salesperson? Why or why not?	What will make you go the extra mile to achieve... ?	What has to happen to put more opportunities in the pipeline?	Who would you really like to have on your side?	What would you say if she said...?

Strategy	Skills & Attitude	Pipeline	Opportunity & Account	Call Planning
What will need to happen before...?	What could you be doing differently to be more effective?	What are you assuming here...? Could another assumption be used...?	How can you get each buying influencer on your side?	Okay, how does that lead to...?
What stands in the way of...?	What would you like to do less of? Why?	What happens if this large deal goes silent?	Is there anything you need from me or the company to...?	What would they need to believe/assume/predict...?
Interesting, tell me more about that...	What has to happen next to work toward... ?	When should we meet to look at your progress on this?	How will the competition try to blow us out of the water? How can you prevent that?	Who will be on the call? Who should be on the call that is not and why?
Which clients do you find most valuable and why?	Are you missing any skills or resources to take the next steps toward your goals?	If we look at your win rate, deal size, and sales cycle, what can you improve?	Who are you talking to? Who should you be talking to? How will they make decisions?	What kind of support can you get from an internal stakeholder in this meeting?
Have you won deals and accounts that you should have stayed away from?	How did your competition outsmart you in the last deal you lost? How can you prevent that this time?	Which stage of the pipeline is the hardest one to move through?	Why would the customer leave the status quo to go with our solution? Why not?	What questions may be asked to shoot you down on this call?

Just as open-ended questions can be incorporated in every area of coaching, so also they can be incorporated into each of the logical levels of change.

Environment	Behavior	Capabilities	Beliefs & Values	Identity	Purpose
Is there anything missing in your environment that would help you perform better?	What actions can you take to improve this part of your performance?	What skills do you need to meet your next set of goals?	What do you need to believe about yourself in order to make progress toward your goals?	How do you describe yourself?	What is your purpose in life?
What else can we do to support you?	Are there actions you should be engaging in more often?	How can you improve the skills you need to achieve this goal?	Were you told things in your childhood that you still believe but that perhaps aren't true?	How would you like others to describe you?	How does your purpose align with what you're doing now?
What aspects of the work environment are holding you back?	What are you doing that may be holding you back?	Are there any capabilities you're lacking that are holding you back?	What beliefs about yourself may be holding you back?	In what ways might who you are be holding you back from who you want to be?	Is there anything holding you back from pursuing your life's purpose?

PROVIDE COACHES WITH INSIGHTS

In order to ask the right questions, coaches need insights about the salespeople from the salespeople themselves, from their systems as well as from customers and coworkers. They need information on each salesperson so that they know who will benefit most from their coaching, and they need information on each deal. Coaches need this information structured so that they can quickly assess who is in need of coaching and in what areas and when. They need visualized data to quickly find out who is falling behind and why, to understand whom to coach and when.

Without this, coaches may focus too much time on the wrong salespeople. For instance, they may spend too much time coaching high performers because it's fun and feels productive or low performers because it feels as if they need it the most. But the truth is, the most effective coaching is often done for the people in the middle who have the most to gain and the best potential to grow.

Likewise, without a good system to provide insights, coaches get stuck asking the same questions over and over again, instead of asking the deeper questions to help salespeople figure out how to get where they want to be.

The process, checklists, and enablement structure defined in the previous chapters provides your coaching system with the framework on which to establish a coaching process that leads to progress, rather than repetition. You can design key questions into the sales process and give coaches insights based on the accurate data that develop out of your team following a consistent process.

The sales process also becomes the structure around which coaches can develop a consistent coaching cadence, so that the coaching doesn't become a fallback behavior that only occurs when there's a problem.

In addition, use your process and enablement to help coaches and salespeople develop a shared language across the organization so that everyone agrees on and knows the definitions for key terms like opportunity, project, and win/loss. Likewise, your process and enablement should support shared key performance indicators (KPIs) that are easy to track and that show trendlines, not just snapshots, so that coaches can see whether salespeople are improving over time and compare their results with set goals.

By providing these tools and resources, you enable coaches to identify bottlenecks and constraints on an individual basis and to coach the right people, at the right time, on the right issues.

MAKE FOLLOW-UP PART OF THE ROUTINE

Train coaches to follow up with salespeople on a routine basis. Every time they meet, they should ask the salesperson about the main issues they agreed upon in the last meeting. Make this easy by providing tracking tools to document the most important takeaways and agreed-upon actions.

PROVIDE TOOLS FOR SELF-COACHING

Time is a significant constraint for most coaches. Enabling salespeople to self-coach saves time for the coach and the salesperson, enables the salesperson to access what they need in a timely fashion, and leaves managers free to coach on matters that salespeople can't coach themselves on.

To enable self-coaching, build training materials, content, goal progression, and feedback into the salesperson's daily workflow. This enables salespeople to pull content that reduces their reliance on their managers for information while empowering them to request coaching when they do need it.

In addition, empower your sales teams to coach each other. Joint deal reviews offer the opportunity for everyone on the team to act as a coach, and when there is a shared language and process, the coaching can remain focused and productive. This type of effort helps to create a productive coaching culture and a continuous learning environment for everyone on the team.

As an added bonus, these activities can be evaluated to help identify who enjoys coaching others and is therefore a prime candidate for management.

Coaching that is built on an effective framework is a critical multiplier that can help your organization achieve far beyond current expectations. It pays to take the time and effort to establish a culture and system that align with your strategy, process, and enablement.

9
HOW TO SUSTAIN AND GROW YOUR COMPETITIVE ADVANTAGE
WITH YOUR WAY OF SELLING

By now, you understand the key elements of the framework that will help your sales organization rise above the rest and achieve world-class performance. Now it's time to bring it all together into your unique way of selling that can become a key differentiating factor for your organization.

In this final chapter, I'm going to show you how to take the principles of this book and support them with technology that empowers you to create and maintain a dynamic Way of Selling that is yours and yours alone—and that grows and develops over time as your organization and market grow and develop.

The right technology can form the platform upon which you build all the rest and enable you to constantly monitor, analyze, update, and optimize your way of selling to ensure you're delivering a buying experience that serves customers so well that they wouldn't dream of buying anywhere else.

I showed you in Chapter Five how current sales technology is failing our industry. By now, you've probably noticed some ways that your current technology stack is going to get in the way of implementing the frameworks in this book.

Let's take a closer look at the problem of technology and then at how to solve it.

THE PROBLEM WITH TECHNOLOGY

Most current sales technology causes two major problems in the sales organization:

- The many-headed Hydra problem, in which technical complexity and customizations cause equally constant breakdowns and work-arounds that interrupt the workflow and create excessive costs

- The point pollution problem, in which dozens of point solutions and plug-ins add up to make the whole less valuable than the sum, as salespeople task-switch constantly and lose productivity in the maze of applications

Both of these problems lead to one even bigger problem: Your sales organization and, especially, the humans in it become the servants of your technology.

That is backward.

When humans are servants to the technology, it inhibits their productivity and effectiveness in a multitude of ways:

- Interrupts their workflow and forces them to constantly task-switch
- Makes it impossible to get into and stay in a state of flow
- Reduces adoption of best practices
- Can represent substantial productivity loss every day
- Represents enormous costs in terms of training and lost time
- Shows how the technology itself becomes an excessive cost burden

This is all so unnecessary.

We should not be the servants of the technology. The technology should be the servant of us.

And that means we have to put technology—including artificial intelligence—in its proper place.

THE SIREN SONG OF AI AND AUTOMATION

In Greek mythology, the Sirens were mermaid-like creatures who sang beautiful songs that attracted the attention of sailors and led them to their doom when they sailed toward the music and dashed their ships upon the rocks.

Artificial intelligence (AI) and automation sing a Siren song of their own to sales organizations right now, as I write this book.

FIG 1.17 Sirens luring sales organizations to their deaths on the rocks.

The marketing industry has seen huge gains by using AI bots and automated sequences to attract and hook new customers and spread the word about brands and even to offer some limited customer service and transactional sales automation.

Many sales professionals and leaders are excited about the promises of AI to help them:

- Reach more people, faster
- Personalize messages without doing the work
- Spend less time prospecting

Unfortunately, complex b2b sales organizations that heed the Siren song of AI may find their metaphorical ships dashed upon the rocks.

If you've ever experienced the frustration of a circular argument with an AI bot while trying to get a question answered about a unique situation, you already intuitively know why complex sales is the wrong place for AI-powered automation.

In complex b2b sales—where human interaction is critical and decisions are made as part of a process, with multiple stakeholders, competing interests, and complex sets of problems and solutions—AI is simply not capable of navigating effectively yet.

And, in fact, when AI is badly implemented (which it usually is), it undermines trust and works against the sales team, often dashing sales before they can be made.

Buyers are inundated with automated messages, thanks to the success of automated marketing. They're saturated and wary of anything that smells remotely like a pitch. A poorly timed or targeted automated message can poison the well, making new prospects more resistant to your efforts and creating friction with existing opportunities.

And don't be fooled by catchwords like hyper-personalization that promise that your automated messages will seem warm and personal to the recipient. We all know, deep in our guts, that it's not true. You can smell a phony "personalized" message a mile from your inbox. Your customers can too.

All of these factors combined—the Hydra problem, the point pollution problem, and the Siren song of AI and automated messaging—have created an environment where our people have become the servants of our machines.

It's time for a new paradigm.

In this new paradigm, your technology serves your people by providing them a solid foundation on which to execute your strategy. It guides them through your process, stores and enables their checklists, reminds them of their training, delivers effective content at the right time in the process, provides access to relevant training and coaching inside their workflow, is beautiful and easy to use, and supports their success as human beings and as world-class sales performers overall.

Instead of artificial intelligence, this technology provides augmented intelligence—augmenting the inherently human and effectively trained intelligence of your sales team, instead of attempting to replace it.

And it all starts by losing our attachment to the big fat Hydras, the point pollution, and the Siren song.

SIMPLIFY AND STREAMLINE YOUR SALES ENABLEMENT TECHNOLOGY

> IF YOU WANT TO TEACH PEOPLE A NEW WAY OF THINKING, DON'T BOTHER TRYING TO TEACH THEM. INSTEAD, GIVE THEM A TOOL, THE USE OF WHICH WILL LEAD TO NEW WAYS OF THINKING.
>
> ~ R. BUCKMINSTER FULLER

I founded and own a Sales Enablement CRM company called Membrain. I envisioned and built this technology because I recognized that current technologies were failing our sales departments. Then we allied ourselves with the sharpest minds in the sales space, partnering to help organizations with commercial strategies, process, and methodology design, training, and coaching.

Everything I'm about to describe to you is built into our technology and supported by our partnerships. You don't have to use Membrain to accomplish most of the benefits of this book, but it is my firm belief that there is no other tool available that will make your process as easy and straightforward as the tool I purpose-built for it.

Membrain got its name because it embodies both the system of records (MEMory) and smart enablement (BRAIN).

The easiest, fastest, and most effective way to execute on the framework outlined in this book is to work with a technology like Membrain that is designed and built to bridge the gap between sales strategy and execution. Such a technology should accomplish these tasks:

- Allow you to visualize an actionable, milestone-based sales process and embed preferred methodology directly into the salesperson's daily CRM workflows
- Educate and guide salespeople through that process and methodology
- Provide separate workflows for logically separate aspects of the sales job, such as prospecting, account management, opportunity, pipeline management, and coaching
- Provide access to relevant training, reminders, and other content inside the workflow, exactly when salespeople need it
- Embed enablement content and collateral in context so that your salespeople easily have the right collateral at their fingertips at the right time
- Hold salespeople accountable to your way of selling with qualifying criteria, guides, and checklists, while also providing autonomy for the individual's creativity
- Visualize each salesperson's goals and progress toward them over time
- Provide managers and coaches with relevant insights and data to genuinely help salespeople improve their skills and approach

- Deliver insights and analytics that enable constant improvement and optimization of both strategy and execution

- Be easy to update and maintain by nontechnical people

- Be simple, beautiful, and easy to use for everyone, requiring minimal task-switching and encouraging a state of flow

The right system will not be weighed down with excess baggage or tools that your team doesn't need or use. It will be built specifically for the complex b2b environment you operate in. And it will be mobile and easy to use on the road, so your salespeople can treat it as home base for everything they do, no matter where they are in the world.

ANALYZE, OPTIMIZE, AND SCALE

With such technology at your disposal and correctly set up to mirror and reinforce your process, methodology, training, enablement, and coaching, you are also well positioned to analyze, optimize, and scale.

The right analytics and dashboards will help you to easily see where your roadblocks, obstacles, and bottlenecks are. Using a technology-supported sales framework also ensures that you're capturing organizational knowledge from your best performers and biggest wins, and using that information to continually optimize your way of selling.

This also enables you to optimize and scale your process across your entire organization, no matter how large, and to propagate new winning behaviors and activities as you become aware of them.

A GREAT WAY TO GROW

The frameworks in this book are designed to help b2b sales organizations thrive and flourish and enjoy the benefits of a healthy, well-trained, well-conditioned, well-enabled team and process.

Apply these principles and frameworks, and you'll not only stop killing deals, you'll win more and have more fun doing it. In other words, you'll stop killing deals.

Why does the framework work so well? Because it honors the essential humanity of the people on your team and the people who constitute your market.

In the story I told at the beginning of this book, I was losing lots of money on a sales team merry-go-round. Today, my world is much different. We've taken on one of the industry's biggest technology companies and become an award-winning competitor. Our technology has been recognized by Top Sales World and G2Crowd for multiple years as one of the industry's leading sales enablement platforms. We're on target to continue growing by impressive numbers year over year.

While we're certainly proud of the technology we've built, our partnerships, and the way we do business, at the core of our success is how we sell.

We don't treat our customers and prospects like interchangeable units in a vast marketplace of machine parts. We treat them like humans, and we respect them as humans. Likewise, we've come to better understand the essential humanity of our sales workforce, and that realization has enabled us to better recruit, train, and support the people on our team to win more deals.

By using the frameworks in this book, and engaging the help of consultants, training companies, and technology providers who can help you execute effectively on it, you too can enjoy radical expansion and the pure thrill of knowing the people on your team and your customers are actually happy, fulfilled human beings.

I think it's a great way to grow.

Now that you have read through this book once, head over to ***https://stop.killing.deals/resources***, and download the resources, if you haven't already done so.

Use the resources there to begin implementing your human-focused frameworks today.

And if you need any help along the way, I would love to hear from you.

READ MORE

1. American Psychological Association, "What You Need to Know about Willpower" https://www.apa.org/helpcenter/willpower

2. Baumeister, Roy, various sources and articles on his research, such as this article from *The Atlantic*: https://www.theatlantic.com/health/archive/2012/04/the-chocolate-and-radish-experiment-that-birthed-the-modern-conception-of-willpower/255544

3. Damasio, Antonio, *Descartes' Error*, 2005 [Chair of Neuroscience and Professor of Psychology, Philosophy, and Neurology at University of Southern California, also cited here: https://www.thecut.com/2016/06/how-only-using-logic-destroyed-a-man.html

4. Dilts, Robert B., *A Brief History of Logical Levels*, NLP University, 2014.

5. Gawande, Atul, "Why Doctors Hate Their Computers", The New Yorker, November 5, 2018.

6. Gawande, Atul, *The Checklist Manifesto*, 2011.

7. Job, Veronika, and colleagues, "Ego Depletion—Is It All In Your Head?" Association for Psychological Science, April 17, 2010.

8. Jordan, Jason. *Cracking the Sales Management Code*, 2011

9. Kahneman, Daniel, *Thinking, Fast and Slow*, 2013

10. Kurlan, Dave, *Baseline Selling*, 2005

11. McMains, Vanessa, "Johns Hopkins study suggests medical errors are a third-leading cause of death in the U.S.," Hub, Johns Hopkins University Magazine, May 3, 2016.

12. Mischel, Walter, various sources on his research, such as this from NPR: https://www.npr.org/sections/health-shots/2018/09/21/650015068/remembrance-for-walter-mischel-psychologist-who-devised-the-marshmallow-test

13. Robertson, Colin, "Why Your Willpower is Like a Muscle—and How to Use It" Willpowered, October 22, 2014.

14. Rosenstock, Irwin M., Victor J. Strecher, and Marshall H. Becker, "Social Learning Theory and the Health Belief Model," Health Education & Behavior, June 1, 1988.

15. Schenk, Tamara, *Sales Enablement: A Master Framework to Engage, Equip, and Empower a World-Class Sales Force* (with Byron Matthews), 2018.

16. Spears, Dean, Princeton University CEPS Working Paper No. 213, December 2010.

17. Farnam Street: "The Spacing Effect: How to Improve Learning and Maximize Retention," https://fs.blog/2018/12/spacing-effect

ACKNOWLEDGMENTS

After deciding to start Membrain.com with the mission to elevate the sales profession, I've had the good fortune of having some amazing people joining me on this journey. This book would not have been possible without their contributions and support. Anders, Henrik, Björn, and all the colleagues at **Membrain**, you all rock!

I also owe gratitude to Patrik, Martin, Ronny, Peter, and the entire team at **Upstream**, the company where the idea for Membrain started. Your quest and work ethics in challenging the mainstream with innovative solutions is impressive and admirable!

Inspiration and ideas for this book have come from my own experiences and the work of thought leaders such as Atul Gawande, Jason Jordan, Sharon Drew Morgen, Neil Rackham, Dave Brock, Dave Kurlan, Shelle Rose Charvet, Bob Apollo, Henrik Larsson-Broman, Kjell Enhager, Magnus Kull, and many more.

As a part of my research for this book, I interviewed authors and thought leaders who were all very kind and generous with their advice and recommendations. Thanks to Andy Paul, Anita Nielsen, Anthony Iannarino, Barbara Weaver-Smith, Brad Childress, Deb Calvert, Joanne Black, John Geraci, Julie Thomas, Ken Valla, Larry Levine, Lee Saltz, Lisa Magnuson, Mark Hunter, Matt Sunshine, Mike Weinberg, Ray Makela, Sheri Levitin, Tamara Shenk, Tim Ohai, Tom Williams, and Trish Bertuzzi. Please forgive me if I have forgotten to mention your name here, as I have surely been inspired by many more great minds.

A special thanks to Fen Druadìn who helps me communicate my thoughts in writing and in English, which isn't my native language. Thanks for working with me and for adding your valuable experience and fantastic personality. Also, a special thanks to Björn for creating the beautiful illustrations for this book and the design of the accompanying website *https://stop.killing.deals/resources*. And a big thank you to Jason Jordan for writing the Foreword.

And, of course, thanks to my wife, Anette, who has been by my side for twenty-eight years and counting. You have always helped me in my endeavors in so many ways. I love you! To Thea and Neo, our children—you inspire me to strive for a better present and future. Always continue to learn, grow, and take action to make life fun, meaningful, and interesting.

ABOUT THE AUTHOR

A lifelong entrepreneur, with twenty years of experience in the software space and a passion for sales and marketing, George Brontén is always looking for new ways to achieve improved business results using innovative software, skills, and processes. He shares his thoughts on the award-winning blog "Art & Science of Complex Sales."

Since 2012, his team at Membrain.com has collaborated with thought leaders and studied research to identify the success factors behind successful sales organizations. The result of their diligence is a Software as a Service that makes it easier for companies to capture, learn, and execute the behaviors needed to achieve sales excellence.

How to contact George Brontén or get more information about Membrain:

* LinkedIn: ***www.linkedin.com/in/georgebronten***
* Twitter: ***https://twitter.com/georgebronten***
* Email: ***george@membrain.com***
* Membrain: ***www.membrain.com***
* Blog: ***www.membrain.com/blog***

Printed in Poland
by Amazon Fulfillment
Poland Sp. z o.o., Wrocław

55501128R00087